70 Activities for Tutor Groups

I don't see why learning has to be boring.
Andrew Taylor, Professor of Politics, University of Huddersfield

70 Activities for Tutor Groups

Peter Davies

Gower

Published by
Gower Publishing Limited
Gower House
Croft Road
Aldershot
Hampshire GU11 3HR
England

Gower
Old Post Road
Brookfield
Vermont 05036
USA

Peter Davies has asserted his right under the Copyright, Designs and Patents Act 1988 to be identified as the author of this work.

British Library Cataloguing in Publication Data
Davies, Peter, 1950–
   70 activities for tutor groups
   1. Group work in education   2. Effective teaching
   3. Classroom management
   I. Title   II. Seventy activities for tutor groups
   371.3'95

ISBN 0 566 08000 1

Library of Congress Cataloging-in-Publication Data
Davies, Peter, 1966–
   70 activities for tutor groups / by Peter Davies.
      p.   cm.
   Includes bibliographical references (p.   ).
   ISBN 0-566-08000-1 (pbk.)
   1. Group work in education. 2. Activity programs in education.
   3. Tutor and tutoring.   I. Title.   II. Title: Seventy activities
   for tutor groups.
   LB1032.D38   1999   99-24994
   371.39'5–dc21   CIP

Typeset in 11/14pt New Baskerville by IML Typographers, Chester and printed in Great Britain by MPG Books Ltd, Bodmin

This book is dedicated to all those tutors who are willing to vary the norm, experiment, and try different teaching strategies in their classes; and also to all those students who are eager to learn, participate and engage themselves in the classroom.

Far better it is to dare mighty things, to win glorious triumphs even though checked by failures than to take rank with those poor spirits who neither enjoy much nor suffer much, because they live in the grey twilight, that knows not, victory or defeat.

Teddy Roosevelt

Contents

Contents

Acknowledgements

This book is the product of research I carried out as part of a Teaching Fellowship study at the University of Huddersfield. I have adapted the original manuscript for this published version, and I now have many people to thank for their help.

First, I would like to thank the University of Huddersfield for facilitating my original study through a very generous Teaching Fellowship grant. I am particularly grateful to Professor Nigel Lemon of the University's Learning Consultancy Group for his help and advice. I was also very appreciative of the support given to me by Professor Brendan Evans, Dean of the School of Music and Humanities. He encouraged me to apply for the Teaching Fellowship and he showed consistent enthusiasm for my project. At Gower Publishing I would like to offer my sincere thanks to Jo Gooderham for all her extremely helpful guidance; she has given me a great deal of confidence and support. May I also express my thanks to Solveig Gardner Servian for all her help.

My research for this study involved scores of interviews, and I must express my most sincere thanks to all the people I interviewed for their time, assistance and general kindness. It was a hugely interesting experience to talk to so many enthusiastic teachers, tutors and students, and I was especially privileged to share their ideas about groupwork. In addition, I found it particularly fascinating to discuss groupwork strategies and techniques with people in other professions: counsellors, trainers and church ministers. I would like to say a special thanks to John Fazey, Mike Murcott, Martin Davies and John Hart. I found the general outlook, and the specific ideas, of these four groupwork specialists to be particularly refreshing and invigorating.

The activities that are codified in this study are a product of the many discussions I had with groupwork practitioners and I have endeavoured to be rigorous with my acknowledgements. Some of the activities I have explained are quite well known and well used; others were passed on to me directly by specific people – and in the following pages I have made it very clear when this has been the case. I have also adapted some techniques from odd, individual comments. In Chapter 4 I have introduced several activities that I first became aware of through existing literature on group-work. Here again, I have made it very clear that I am citing other people's work, and I have quoted the relevant source. At this juncture I would like to point out that the propaganda posters used in Chapter 1 were taken from Anthony Rhodes' excellent book, *Propaganda: The Art of Persuasion*, published by Angus & Robertson and edited by Victor Margolin, which is no longer in print.

Many of the quotations and comments used in this study were taken directly from questionnaire forms very kindly completed by students and tutors. I need to thank all the questionnaire respondents for their time, honesty and very provocative opinions!

Strenuous efforts have been made to gain copyright clearance for certain tables, illustrations and passages of text that have been used in this book. The author apologises most sincerely if, inadvertently, any copyright has been infringed.

I also want to thank Marilyn Pursglove, Linda Franklin and Lisa Cox for taking on a portion of my teaching commitments while I was researching this project. They were particularly conscientious and dedicated in fulfilling their duties. They were also kind enough to read parts of this script and offered many helpful suggestions.

I fervently hope that I have acknowledged everyone whose help needs to be acknowledged. I apologize profusely to anyone who feels I have not acknowledged their ideas. I have made every effort to do so.

I would also like to thank the following people: Jackie Beedle (massive secretarial help), Martin Davies (substantial help with various aspects of the book), Derek Lynch (many helpful suggestions and general computer assistance), Colin McCaig (questionnaire distribution), Martin Evans-Jones (contacts in North Wales), Robert Davies (contacts and other help) and John Williams (the morning in Pudsey). Finally, I am very grateful to the following people for their constructive comments about specific chapters of this study: Rhys Davies, Janet Conneely, Martin Davies and my mum!

Peter Davies

Introduction

This book is an attempt to bring together the enormous variety of groupwork activities on offer to teachers and tutors. It is intended to be an easy-to-use, reader-friendly guide, designed particularly for those who teach arts, humanities or social science subjects (or any other discussion-based subjects).

Of course, in many circumstances the tutor can stimulate discussion through his or her own skills and personality – subtle interjections, challenging comments and even humour. However, at other times even the most charismatic teacher can struggle. It is on such occasions that a 'tool kit' of techniques for teaching and learning is helpful, and perhaps even essential. This is the central concern of the book. It seeks to advance a full kaleidoscope of possible classroom activities for use by tutors. The fundamental question is this: how can classroom sessions be changed and varied for the better?

The need, essentially, is for more purposeful participation and involvement, and even for more fun! Whatever the philosophy, the ultimate aim of all groupwork practitioners is effective learning and – to use current jargon – meaningful learning outcomes. This book, therefore, attempts to outline and explain a range of interesting and stimulating groupwork activities.

Parts I and II outline a repertoire of activities, all of which are explained with the aid of exemplars; the aim of each activity is to generate effective small-group discussion (all activities are explained as if they are to be employed in a discussion group of 12 students). Part I presents techniques by type or genre, while Part II investigates three areas in which tutors often give up trying to make their teaching creative and imaginative: namely, abstract ideas, primary documents and numerical data. The message to emerge from both sections is that good, healthy discussion *can* be stimulated via imaginative groupwork activities.

The reader should note that each activity is usually explained with reference to one worked-through example. Where the activity involves a graphic element, the 'diagram' is usually a would-be student effort; here, the underlying hope is that even just one 'attempt' – however imperfect – will provoke debate among a small student group, with each participant eager to explain why he or she either agrees or disagrees with the image under the spotlight. By necessity the 'examples' used are short and snappy and designed to help the reader understand exactly how the activity works. Obviously, too, there is a strong element of transferability; so, if the worked-through example comes from one subject area (e.g. history), the activity should work equally well in another subject area (e.g. English).

It should also be stressed that the timeframes mentioned – for example, five minutes (introduction); 15 minutes (small-group work); 10 minutes (whole-group plenary) – are only suggestions and, obviously, teachers and tutors should use their discretion on this matter throughout. The 'variation' ideas included in the write-up of each activity are also only suggestions; they can be used when and where appropriate. The 'cross references' are included to aid tutors further in their choice of activities. Throughout, the underlying aim is to encourage tutors to be imaginative in their teaching, and to put a special emphasis on variety and variation.

At this juncture the very nature and rationale of activities as catalysts must be considered. Many critics attack the very idea of activities. Some strategies are condemned as 'artificial', 'mechanical', 'shallow' or 'childish'. The central argument put forward in this book, however, is that activities are a 'means' – a means to the end of stimulating and catalysing classroom discussion. In very *realpolitik* terms, the end can, and does, justify the means. If, as the product of classroom activity, student discussion is good, healthy and buoyant, the nature of the method used is irrelevant. And, obviously, from good classroom discussion can come effective learning and understanding – the ultimate end and goal.

In outlining and explaining a selection of groupwork activities, I have made a special point of stating that whole-group discussion can and should follow on, normally and naturally, from each and every one. It is obvious too that students will be engaging each other in discussion as the activity is actually *in operation*. The techniques in this handbook are proven and do work and the comments in the following section testify to this. As a community, teachers and tutors *should not* be too proud; they *should* be ready to pool ideas and they *should* be encouraged to utilize different activities, in order to promote discussion, when and where appropriate.

An array of literature obviously exists on the subject of teaching, teaching strategy and teaching methods. Much of this, however, centres on educational theory, and even the more practical guides – extremely helpful though they are – tend to be quite generalized and more concerned with hints and advice than specific worked-through subject-orientated examples (see References and further reading). Thus, particularly in the realm of arts, humanities and social science subjects, there is perhaps no accessible 'hands-on' guide for teachers who want to vary their groupwork tactics. I aim to address this apparent deficiency head-on in the forthcoming pages.

All the activities codified in this book have their place, and also their potential. They are certainly not set in stone, so the interested reader can vary and play around with them to meet specific classroom needs. In a sense, the activities can only really be judged 'in action'. On paper they may sound sensible and well thought out; in action – with added energy – they can really come alive.

Quote, unquote

Small-group discussion is an important part of all pupils' and all students' lives. But it is clear that there are a variety of approaches towards classroom learning. This section incorporates a whole range of views on small-group work – those of university tutors and school teachers, but also the testimonies of counsellors, trainers, church ministers and workshop specialists. It explores attitudes to groupwork from a series of different perspectives and catalogues the opinions of a variety of practitioners.

There is an onus on us to ensure that every student gets something out of a group session. (Professor Stephen George, Professor of Politics, University of Sheffield)

*I suppose that you should throw in as much funky fun and activity as possible to break up the monotony – **and** because people learn better this way. But I feel we do still have to cater for people of a more traditional background.* (Christine Bell, Learning Consultancy Group, University of Huddersfield)

I always like to break things up. With groups of 14 it's always good to create small groups, with each group preparing different things, or even similar things. It's very healthy to hear students' different perspectives. (Dr Geoff Cubitt, Lecturer in History, University of York)

I definitely feel that there is an onus on staff to vary things. I don't think tutors should forcefully set the agenda. Sometimes, for example, where there are four main points to cover, I'd rather do two or three in detail than have to do the set four. (Dr Rebecca Bryson, Tutor in History, University of Huddersfield)

Groups work best when people know each other. When people have got to know each other, you can then take things forward. It's like a journey. People need to feel comfortable with each other, so they can talk with each other and not get laughed at. People must feel secure, so they can go on to discuss controversial issues. (Rev. Inderjit Bhogal, Urban Theology Unit, Sheffield)

Students at root are not used to intellectual discussion. It's Oxford and Cambridge who get the students who are used to intellectual discussion. (Professor Andrew Taylor, Professor of Politics, University of Huddersfield)

As to the structure of groupwork sessions, I think you can either let the group members know beforehand or you can keep things spontaneous. If you do let people know beforehand, they might start to think or worry about forthcoming exercises, but on the other hand, if you do air the agenda right at the start, people can think about how they're going to approach exercises. Tutors have got to have a remote control and act almost like the choreographer. (Martin Davies, Former SCM Northern Regional Secretary)

I like to give students specific reading – from the tutorial pack, short-term loan or from photocopies. I like them to read and then do a mini-presentation. This is good but it's also still a little constricting. I want to recommend reading, but I also want them to use their own initiative. (Janet Conneely, Tutor in History, University of Huddersfield)

There is a common myth: the educator is always in control, at the helm and in charge of a body of information. As long as this is the case you've done your job.... But the truth is that just because you're speaking and talking, it doesn't mean students understand. With new strategies and new activities there's always staff resistance to some extent. Students really get put on the line: the resistant staff say students aren't learning through the new methods, but you have to respond by saying that perhaps they're learning better. (Maggie Sheen, Deputy Head and English Teacher, Pudsey Grangefield High School)

The focus for this department's teaching is the seminar and one-to-one or one-to-two staff/ student tutorials. Students can gain a lot from small-group activity, from the interaction and from the seminar leader. But there's a big variety in delivery. It's the core of our process – to make students exact in the ideas they develop and in their general understanding. (Dr Allen Warren, Lecturer in History, University of York)

Interactive learning is in vogue – as is experiential learning. Older people generally resist groupwork. They say things like 'This is a waste of my time'. They feel vulnerable when they're engaged in groupwork. It's easy to resist – because groupwork is quite threatening. I do feel that groupwork practitioners have to be aware of this. Groupwork activities do need to mean some-thing. Learning has to be extracted at the end. Activities are, often, not specifically designed for learning, so the learning aspects have to be driven home at the end. (Rev. Sue Havens, Angli-can Chaplain, University of Manchester)

Small-group training is a very effective method of development. Issues can be raised in a sensi-tive way. You can be flexible – but there have to be ground rules. You have to encourage people to opt in. (Rev. Rowland Goodwin, Methodist Minister, Sale, Manchester)

For us, involvement and activity means learning. This activity and participation might involve teamwork, case-study work or the students actually writing on the board themselves. (Mike Haines, Head of Business Studies, Tytherington High School, Macclesfield)

I'm not happy with chalk and talk – but students do like having an outline. ... It is important to offer a variety of methods. (Paul Bound, History Teacher, Pudsey Grangefield High School)

It's a good tactic to break up time to incorporate various skills – reading, listening, discussion, graphic skills. In turn the learning outcomes are broken down and are various. (Professor Nigel Lemon, Learning Consultancy Group, University of Huddersfield)

I found that work in small groups promoted good discussion, healthy criticism and often allowed a shy, reserved pupil an opportunity to speak in a more relaxed situation. The tradi-tional method of teaching, involving the teacher facing rows of desks and delivering informa-tion, is very much a one-way process, where the pupil absorbs information or, significantly, fails to take part in the process. (Penny Watts, Maths and Music Teacher, Warrington)

I am warm to doing different things – but there is a big cost in time, especially where handout production is involved. We don't want to spoon-feed but, rather, provide students with the materials they need to enter into the academic argument. Debate is fundamental. (Dr Bill Roberts, Principal Lecturer in History, University of Huddersfield)

When I did teacher training the importance of discussion and participation was really stressed. The notion was that learning did not take place in lectures, but in involvement, participation, discussion and feedback. After all, there's no big retention rate with listening. Younger people in particular find it difficult to retain information and need more involvement. (Rhys Davies, History Teacher, Tytherington High School, Macclesfield)

Variety is the key – giving students different things to focus on. You've got to keep students' interest – even with the 6th form. Pre-GCSE learning is very student-centred – with students split up to concentrate on activities. (Illy Adam, Head of Business Studies, Pudsey Grangefield High School)

As a tutor I have recognized students' need to feel important. They like to be picked to do jobs and play roles. When I give them a job, it's as if they are asking: 'Why did she pick me?' I have enjoyed creating small groups with people talking, and then talking to me. This breaks the silence. Silence is an awful thing. You shouldn't be under the grill, having to know the answer. (Linda Franklin – Tutor in History, University of Huddersfield)

It is better when group sessions are more relaxed and informal. There is a world of pomposity in universities – and you can often really not feel like contributing. Things need to be far more down-to-earth and less pompous. It's as if academics think they have the key to academia – as if there is a kind of cloak surrounding academic life. (Heather Pindar, Former German and European Studies Student, University of Sussex (1985–89))

Devices can relax and open up people. They can work. I'm not against doing different things in a given hour but the logistics mean you've only really got half an hour to play with. There's also the preparation time; this can add to the logistical problems. With different exercises there's so little time. Students, in addition, absorb so very little. Time is precious, and any efforts to seg-mentize can be sabotaged by students. (Dr Derek Lynch, Lecturer in Politics, University of Huddersfield)

I enjoy work with small groups, but I know that if I attempted to break my Sunday congregation up into small groups a lot of them probably wouldn't come to church again. I prefer to experiment with group sessions during the week – encounter groups. Here there is a lot of potential for small-group work. (Rev. Robert Davies, Methodist Minister, Buxton)

Activity can relax people and validate what they think and believe is good. It helps them in a non-threatening way. For children, activities are quite natural – playing with bricks and the like. You can set up all kinds of creative activities. You need activity. Everyone grows through this – you're engaged physically as well as mentally. Making, doing, interacting. . . . You also need a variety of listening, doing and talking. I think you have to keep sitting and listening to a minimum. Kids are more instinctive and they'll tell you when they're bored! Facilitating people is the key. You need to give them confidence to speak. (Christine Wright, Scripture Union, Bletchley, Milton Keynes)

We must give responsibility to students – asking them to think, talk and contribute in a focused way to the debate. They must put forward testable arguments. We also have to remember that the dynamics of groups differ according to the people and the personalities and characters involved. The personality of the teacher is very important, and there are many variables that affect things. It's about the chemistry evident in the class – students must be brought in. (Dr Philip Woodfine, Principal Lecturer in History, University of Huddersfield)

I like pupils to be able to touch, feel and look at visual material and pictures in the classroom situation. Visual stimuli are important, especially for the younger children. Cartoons, for example, are brilliant sources. I am very conscious of having teaching devices and of splitting my lessons into segments. It is almost second nature, and I do try to vary things as much as possible. Doing things is very active – otherwise things can be very passive. (Christine Stead, Deputy Head and History Teacher, Brooksbank School, Elland, Halifax)

I think we have a duty to teach transferable skills, and to encourage and develop oral skills. Groupwork and role-play can be linked to oral skills development – creating cooperative exercises within the discussion. We do have an onus to increase student involvement and student activity. (Dr Bill Stafford, Principal Lecturer in Politics, University of Huddersfield)

Whatever the tool or the method you must ask yourself: 'Do students latch onto it?' 'Is it successful?' I say: 'If it works, do it!' You can always represent things in a different way. If students show understanding, the method is justified! It doesn't really matter what the tactic is. Simple things can also be very subtle. All this is perhaps ignored by the traditional approach. Activity without purpose is just activity. We must choose the appropriate tools to help people conceptualize. The results are important but so is the process: the means and the tools. (Mike Murcott, Training Advisory Service, Buxton)

It would be easy to criticize new devices: they are artificial, but they can be effective and often preferable. There is a strong argument for variation and artificial techniques. Some of these techniques work. You do, though, have to have a different approach to different groups. (Professor Brendan Evans, Professor of Politics, University of Huddersfield)

I believe that a person's intelligence should not be a barrier to doing activities. I would argue that you should always be willing to do yourself what you do with your kids in classes. To have a room full of students – maybe 150 in a lecture hall – and not to involve them is a big waste of intellect. There shouldn't just be one person working and thinking. Things have got to be hands-on. (Julian Cooper, Geography Teacher, Tytherington High School, Macclesfield)

All in all, groupwork teaching is not a science, and you've got to have flexibility. We are after all dealing with human beings and I think you have to be flexible, and adapt things where necessary. With devices I think you need to be clear about the aim and meaning of the exercise, and I do think you have to summarize things at the end. (Judith Ashurst, Relate, Huddersfield)

I think that schoolteachers vary things in their classes because of pupils' attitude and, in general, because of pupil demand. The children can't cope with very formal teaching, and anyway classes are mixed ability, so you have got to make an effort to get everybody involved. Most pupils are not prepared just to sit there and listen. (Jenny Hussein, Head of History, Tytherington High School, Macclesfield)

At school we had better teachers than we did at university. At school, just in English, we did role-play, drama, acting, handiwork, craftwork, visual representation, and we also watched videos and listened to music clips. We did all manner of practical exercises. (Martin Davies, former SCM Northern Regional Secretary, Manchester)

I was at Ruskin College, Oxford and there was very little variation in teaching style. (Dr Martin Cloonan, Case Studies, Department of Politics, University of York)

When I was at college I was generally just talked at. (Jill Leckey, Senior Lecturer in Mental Health, University of Huddersfield)

There seems to be no doubt that small-group work is a good and beneficial thing: it is personal, informal and can become highly stimulating. This book aims to supply teachers and tutors with a quick and easy-to-use guide to 70 practical and imaginative small-group activities, all of which can be effective in provoking constructive, relevant and meaningful classroom discussion, thus enhancing learning and understanding. Please use the book as a resource and a menu – to choose from selectively.

Part I

Activities – by genre

In this Part – comprising Chapters 1–5 – a range of groupwork approaches are introduced, explained and analysed. Arranged by generic type, the activities considered have several common characteristics: they are all proven and workable (I have pooled the ideas and experiences from over 60 interviews!); they all stand as quick and easy-to-use discussion-provokers; and they all aim to bring participation, involvement and effective learning to groupwork sessions.

No doubt some of the activities will be more popular than others: some people will like some, some people will like others. Others will undoubtedly be passed over as 'not my cup of tea'. The point is that these activities work – they are imaginative, creative and they are a means to the end of stimulating effective group discussion, so choose the ones which suit your particular situation and which work for you.

1 Display

We live in a very visual age. When students see something it brings the idea alive a bit more. They can't get away from it. They've got to deal with it and face it.
Janet Conneely, Tutor in History, University of Huddersfield

Introduction

However much visual potential some topics have, classroom sessions continue to remain arenas where linear text and verbalization are dominant. Often, though, students need high levels of confidence, or a helpful 'hand up', before they feel comfortable enough to speak fluently, and it is in this context that non-verbal stimuli can provoke and catalyse excellent discussion and debate.

This chapter outlines a series of teaching methods, all of which involve an element of display. In most cases, the aim is to inspire students to comment on, and analyse, provocative visual material – posters, slogans or some other kind of visual image – pinned to the classroom wall. It is amazing in fact how the mere action of displaying a poster or a slogan on the wall can stir students into meaningful discussion. As such, this is a simple but effective classroom tactic.

In general, we can note two main types of learning strategy. First, and most obviously, tutors can expose students to powerful visual material. Here the tactic is to either provoke, perplex, involve or even shock! Whatever the response, students will be forced to reflect and think. Discussion *can* be stimulated by displayed visual material, and barriers to verbalization *can* be broken down.

A second strategy follows a converse path. Why not ask students to create their own visual images? It is a fact that many people 'think' in pictorial or graphic form. It is also true that diagrams, graphic representations, and even slogans, can simplify and clarify difficult and complex ideas. Good discussion can also take place between students as their creative efforts evolve from embryonic form to full life. In addition, once thoughts and ideas are 'externalized' in this visual way, they can often become more real and more malleable. So, why not use student-produced graphics to promote understanding, facilitate learning and provoke further discussion?

I would like to thank Martin Davies, Janet Conneely, Geoff Cubitt and Rhys Davies for passing on ideas for this chapter.

Related activities

The following activities, outlined and explained in other chapters, also include an important 'display' element:

1

Spin doctors

In a nutshell

Improve understanding and stimulate debate on a set organization or movement by asking students, in pairs, to act as advertising executives or marketing advisers (or even spin doctors!) and to present or sell it in graphic form through an image, a symbol, a slogan or even a logo.

Aims

1. To simplify and clarify the key aspects and elements of a significant organization.
2. To stimulate debate and discussion on a set topic or issue.
3. To tap into students' artistic skills and enable them to express their thoughts and feelings non-verbally.
4. To enfranchise those participants who might find whole-group debate difficult.
5. To emphasize the nature and role of marketing.

What is needed

- Felt-tip marker pens.
- Sheets of A4 paper.
- Blu-tack.

Time required

10 minutes (design) plus 10 minutes (discussion).

How it works

The students in the group are paired up and given felt-tip pens, paper and Blu-tack. They are asked to exchange thoughts and ideas, and then to create an image, symbol or logo to represent the organization or movement under consideration. After ten minutes, all the graphic efforts are fixed to the wall, and a short discussion ensues. What is the most dominant idea in the images? What is the overall verdict on the organization as represented in the graphics?

A good example in action: Economics – the World Bank

The World Bank goes on a publicity offensive; it needs to improve its image across the globe. Student sub-groups are set the task of marketing the organization in words and slogans. Ideas include the following:

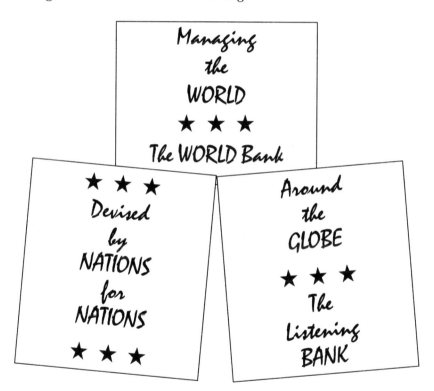

What issues do these advertising efforts raise? What is the main thread of the marketing ideas? How would the governments of the world and the international economic community respond?

Advantages of this activity

1. It makes students think about image and publicity.
2. It enables students to express themselves creatively.

Potential problem

When asked to produce images or logos, students habitually say they 'can't draw' – this barrier must be overcome!

Main learning outcomes

Students are given the opportunity to discuss the nature and characteristics of the organization both in pairs and in the whole group. They will be able to learn about the key features of the movement under consideration, and they will realize the importance, potency and potential of 'image'.

Variation

I like the idea of students translating one form of source into another form. This could mean seeing an image or artefact, and then writing an equivalent source – putting the visual into words. This might mean seeing a Nazi propaganda poster, for example, and then writing a Nazi statement to embody the visual image. This can also obviously be done in reverse – reading a text and producing some kind of visual image to represent it.

At the end of the class the teacher can reveal all! If the students have been writing, he or she can reveal a typical Nazi text; if they've been creating posters, a genuine Nazi poster can be shown. With both strategies, students have to think and empathize – and the teacher can tie it up nicely at the end.

Rhys Davies, History Teacher, Tytherington High School, Macclesfield

2

Gallery

In a nutshell

This is the ultimate visual strategy! The idea is to make the classroom into a gallery, with visual material dominating all the walls. This activity is particularly effective when the visual material is posters (propaganda posters, for example). Big posters are difficult to look at without using the full space and potential of the classroom walls. So why not exploit this potential? When the gallery has been created, send students around it.

Aims

1. To show off visual material that might otherwise go unexploited.
2. To identify the significant features of the posters – whether images or words.

What is nccdcd

●   A gallery of posters or other visual images to display.
●   A pad of Post-it notes.
●   Felt-tip marker pens.

Time required

15 minutes (for the gallery tour) plus 15 minutes (whole-group discussion).

How it works

The posters or other visual images are displayed, and students are asked to tour the gallery in pairs. With Post-it notes in hand they are encouraged to identify key images or words on the posters – jotting down their points on the Post-it notes, and sticking these on the posters in appropriate places. A plenary session follows, with the teacher chairing a discussion about each poster, and the students explaining their thoughts and engaging in relevant discussion. For example, why are the posters so poignant? What features of the posters are most significant?

A good example in action: History – Soviet propaganda during the Second World War

Source: Rhodes (1976, pp. 225–40)

Advantages of this activity

1. The atmosphere of the session is refreshingly different – students can stand up and walk round!
2. Very important points and themes can emerge from visual sources.

Potential problem

Students may use the 'walking round' aspect of this exercise as an excuse to chat with their friends and not concentrate on the task in hand!

Main learning outcomes

Students will be stimulated and engaged by the visual material, and discussion, both in the pairs and in the whole-group will be provoked.

Variations

1. Gibbs (1992, pp. 13–14) explains a similar idea: 'Poster tours'. Here the outcomes of small-group discussions are represented on blank posters. One student per group is asked to stay by their poster and explain it to other students who are touring the classroom; a blank poster can be pinned up next to each group's poster for constructive graffiti.
2. Hounsell, McCulloch and Scott (1996, p. 95) introduce the 'Group poster presentation': small student groups 'are given five weeks in which to work on this project ... and they are required to present their work in the form of a poster during a presentation session to both staff and students'.

3

___

Family trees

In a nutshell

Comprehend and clarify the make-up and lineage of a social, economic or historical tradition via student-designed posters. Ask groups of students to produce a diagrammatic 'family tree' for the designated tradition, and use the 'trees' as a basis for a whole-group discussion.

Aims

1. To simplify and comprehend important and perhaps complex lineages.
2. To liberate those students who can express themselves best, and most naturally, in visual, non-verbal form.
3. To emphasize the fact that genealogies are often interesting, controversial and subjective.

What is needed

*   Felt-tip marker pens.
*   A3 paper.
*   Blu-tack.

Time required

20 minutes (small-group work on the graphic) plus 15 minutes (whole-group discussion).

How it works

The tutor identifies and introduces the tradition or lineage under discussion. The students are broken up into groups of three (no more!) and each group is asked to produce a family tree diagram to represent, and also to simplify, the key tradition. The completed diagrams are posted on the classroom wall, and these posters form the basis of a whole-class discussion.

A good example in action: RE – Where does the modern Methodist Church come from?

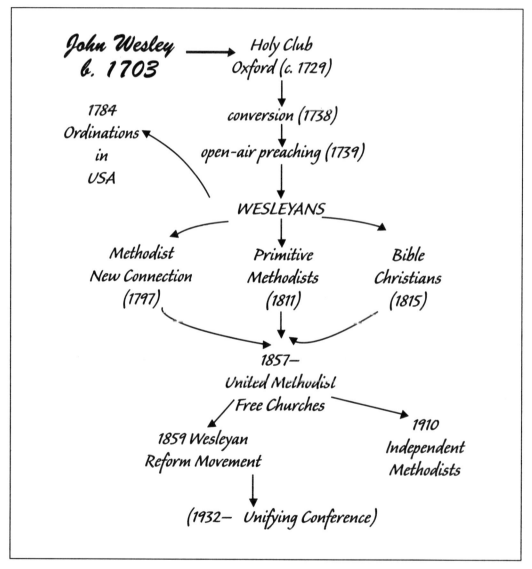

What issues does this family tree raise? How accurate is it? How could it be improved?

Advantages of this activity

1.	Diagrams can clarify important issues and relationships.
2.	Students have to think incisively about how to represent the key points and issues.
3.	There is ample time to discuss the family tree 'process', and the main issues to come out of it, in the small- and whole-group contexts.

Potential problem

To diagrammatize anything – let alone a complex social, political or historical genealogy – is a potentially awkward task; students should be reassured that all approaches are valid.

Main learning outcomes

Students will be able to explore a key tradition, and many of its intricacies, and will also be challenged to represent their ideas diagrammatically.

Variation

The 'family tree' idea is just one way of using diagrams to explain and explore important issues. There is also the 'time-chart' concept, whereby students are asked to represent an important, and perhaps problematic, chronology in the form of a graphic, with all key dates and events represented and explained.

4

Caption competition

In a nutshell

Turn the usual classroom routine on its head! Give students two or three visual sources to look at – but withhold all the captions.

Aims

1.   To engage students more fully in visual analysis.
2.   To inject a 'guessing game' element into groupwork discussion.
3.   To stimulate students through competition and a game-style classroom format.

What is needed

●   Visual images (with their captions cut off!).
●   A4 paper.
●   Felt-tip marker pens.

Time required

10 minutes (for analysing images and creating captions) plus 15 minutes (revelation of answers and whole-group discussion).

How it works

Students, in small sub-groups, are given a set of images to study, analyse and caption.

The images might be cartoons, posters or something else. All the captions are cut off or Tippexed out. The students have to discuss and evaluate the sources and imagine or predict what captions would be appropriate for what images.

Each subgroup then writes its new captions on separate sheets of A4 paper. The tutor chairs the plenary discussion, and each image is considered in turn. The groups' different caption ideas for each are put up on the wall. The various predictions are discussed and the tutor reveals the real caption! Which group is closest? What crucial features and meanings does each image possess?

A good example in action: History – Hitler tears up the Nazi–Soviet Pact

Source: Daily Mail, 23 June 1941, reprinted in Laver, 1993.

1. What is Hitler saying in the speech bubble? (Answer: 'Forgive me, comrade, but it seemed such a good opportunity'.)
2. What is the caption to this cartoon? (Answer: 'Forgive me comrade'.) (Laver, 1993, p. 55)

Students have to discuss these two questions sensibly and intelligently.

Advantages of this activity

1. It puts the onus on students to 'read' the images.
2. Prediction games create very healthy competition and rivalry.
3. It's good fun – and it will create a stir!

Potential problem

This can be quite a difficult exercise to complete successfully without guidance – some clues from the tutor might be in order!

Main learning outcomes

Students will be encouraged to think about, analyse and decode important visual images, and they will engage in a focused classroom discussion.

5

Society diagrams

In a nutshell

Enliven discussions of class, status and society by diagrammatizing society – depicting all the main groupings and the key relationships at stake. Round the exercise off with a feedback session. What main points emerge from the diagrams? How do they add to, or change, our conception and perception of society?

Aims

1. To vary the standard approach – and complement verbal tactics with non-verbal tactics.
2. To encourage students to think about society in new, fresh and stimulating diagrammatic ways.

What is needed

- A3 paper.
- Felt-tip marker pens.
- Blu-tack.

Time required

15 minutes (drawing of the diagram) plus 10 minutes (whole-group discussion).

How it works

In the midst of a group discussion about society or social history a 'time-out' is called: students form into pairs and are asked to represent the state of society in graphic, diagrammatic terms, using circles, arrows and whatever else to clarify what they see as the main conflicts, issues or themes at play. The paired-up students will be able to engage in discussion as they think about and draw their diagram, and also share their ideas and conceptions in a whole-group plenary session.

A good example in action: Sociology – contemporary British society

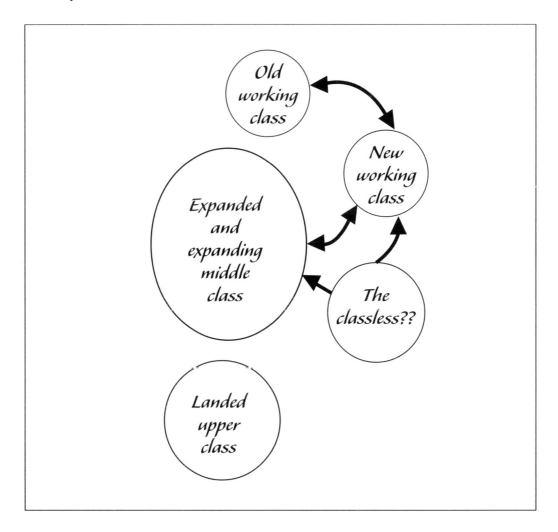

How effective is this particular diagram in representing British society? What are the relationships between the different groups? What do the arrows represent? What does this diagram say about the nature of British society? What are the main themes? How could the diagram be made more accurate?

18

Advantages of this activity

1. By simplifying points in diagrammatic form, difficult issues and relationships can be clarified.
2. Students are challenged! For instance, in the above example, how do you represent the working class – and, say, its resentments – in graphic form?

Potential problem

Students might feel there is one right way to represent society in graphic form – but there obviously isn't!

Main learning outcomes

Students will consider, think through and analyse the mechanics of society – as they see them – and will be able to engage in focused discussion on the different conceptualizations of society.

Variations

If the complexities of society can be represented in diagrammatic form so can a multitude of other related topics – for example, the workings of government, the intricacies of the parliamentary process, multi-party political systems, international diplomatic relationships. With a little imagination, any situation or process can be diagrammatized, and this challenge to students will automatically provoke good, healthy discussion.

6

Visual sources

In a nutshell

In all subjects, sources are usually written and linear. Too often perhaps, tutors neglect to vary the type of material presented to students. With this activity the emphasis is on non-written and non-linear stimuli.

Aims

1. To stimulate students via non-orthodox sources, and to liberate those who find written sources either problematic or routine.
2. To vary the skills that students are required to use – from reading to seeing and interpreting.
3. To catalyse discussion around the visual sources.

What is needed

Photocopies of the visual material.

Time required

10 minutes (pairwork) plus 15 minutes (whole-group discussion)

How it works

A simple format: paired-up students are allocated visual sources to study, analyse and discuss. They jot down the main points and themes that 'jump out' at them from the sources. A whole-group discussion about each image follows, with each pair contributing on the following questions:

- How can the image be described and explained?
- How and why was it produced?
- What are the most obvious or important aspects of the image?
- What themes emerge from it?
- What are the consequences or implications of the image?

A good example in action: History – Second World War propaganda

↑ AMERICAN POSTER

↑ JAPANESE PROPAGANDA IN FAVOUR OF JAPAN–PHILIPPINES SOLIDARITY

US RECRUITING POSTER IN COMIC-STRIP STYLE
→

Source: Rhodes (1976, pp. 150, 253, 258).

What is the significance of these sources?

Advantages of this activity

1. It varies the standard approach.
2. It encourages students to think in new and different ways.
3. It exposes students to an array of different, powerful and important sources.
4. Visual sources, when they are employed, tend to deformalize classroom sessions with many associated benefits.

Potential problem

Students may be a little lax, lazy or non-rigorous in their image analysis, because they may not perceive the visual sources to be on a par with the more standard, written type of source in terms of importance and significance.

Main learning outcomes

Students will become familiar with an array of visual sources, and discussion will have been provoked on key topics.

Variations

Written sources can be complemented by other types of visual stimuli: cartoons, paintings, photographs, posters, images, graphs, diagrams and other sorts of non-linear stimulus.

7

Artefacts

In a nutshell

'Touching' and 'feeling' are two ways of learning that do not seem to be emphasized at college level. Indeed, it is rare for tutors to bring in props or artefacts to any classes. Yet the fact is that 'seeing' things, 'feeling' things and 'touching' things can be a good way to learn and an excellent, very spontaneous, stimulus to discussion.

Aims

1. To bring subjects alive via artefacts.
2. To expose students to authentic and possibly problematic material.
3. To catalyse discussion around the evidence of artefacts.

What is needed

Artefacts to consider!

Time required

10 minutes (small-group discussion of artefacts) plus 15 minutes (whole-group discussion).

How it works

Very simply, artefacts can be handed out to small student subgroups around the room. It is up to each group to consider and analyse their artefact and for the leader of each group to note down the main points of interest about it on a piece of card. The artefacts are then circulated around the room in a clockwise direction, with each group making notes, on separate pieces of card, about the artefacts it receives. When all the artefacts have been passed round the full circle, the tutor chairs a discussion about each object, with each group contributing its specific thoughts on each. A general plenary-style discussion can follow.

A good example in action: Politics – *Front National* boutique paraphernalia *c*.1990

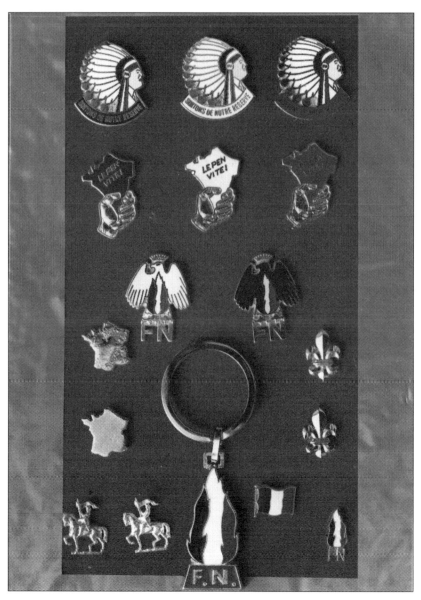

What is the message behind the keyring and badges?

Advantages of this activity

1. Students are exposed to real, concrete, authentic evidence, and not merely expected to engage in abstract verbalization.
2. It gives ample opportunity for discussion in both small- and whole-group contexts.

Potential problem

Students might fail to take the artefacts seriously – and might consequently regard the whole session as just a cop-out.

Main learning outcomes

Students will be exposed to various artefacts and will be encouraged to both discuss their observations and relate the evidence of the artefacts to that contained in more conventional texts and documents.

Summary and evaluation

Throughout their university life students are expected to verbalize, conceptualize and intellectualize, even though they might have very little training in these skills and find it unnatural and difficult to commit themselves to these tasks. Of course, in the end, students' essays and assignments are assessed on their intellectual coherency and their analytical depth, but surely tutors have a responsibility to pro voke and enable conceptualization in new ways, especially where less able students are concerned.

Tutors should not be frightened to introduce more graphic, visual or creative exercises into their group sessions. Nor should they be embarrassed by 'felt-tip culture'. Rather, they should be fully aware that the use of pictorial representation and diagrams is an imaginative and often beneficial strategy, whatever the context – whether it is assessing a key relationship, explaining a crucial process, under-standing a key idea or theory, or representing the *raison d'être* of an event or an organization.

Furthermore, the beauty of visual strategies is their economy. A five-minute exercise can, potentially, help students grasp and understand an extremely difficult and complex topic. It can also help provoke, catalyse and stimulate excellent debate, with discussion centring around the externalized images produced by students or the set visual images under consideration. Complicated topics can be simplified via the use of images and diagrams, and further understanding can then follow. It should also be remembered that a significant proportion of students do learn in a visual and graphic way. Diagrams and images can be a crucial 'way-in' to a topic. They can certainly unlock doors.

Tutors should not be neglectful of visual methods; nor should they underestimate their power. Of course, visual methods have their critics: they are deemed 'shallow', 'superficial' and 'flawed', especially where they are promoted as some form of 'short-cut'. But the fact remains that many students find it far more natural to express themselves in graphic form than in words, and external or externalized images can be a superb catalyst for debate.

2 Games

Games can be interesting and revealing. At the end of a game, people realize why it was being used.
Mike Murcott, Training Advisory Service, Buxton

Introduction

Most people involved in education agree that learning should be enjoyable, exciting, and, yes, fun! However, this aspect does perhaps get lost amid the routine and formality of study. One of the most obvious ways to engender fun, and thus promote interest in a subject and further discussion of it, is to incorporate either games, puzzles or quizzes into teaching.

With learning aims in mind, it should be pointed out that games, puzzles and quizzes, as a legitimate teaching tactic, do contain two vital ingredients: first, competition or rivalry between students – always a healthy addition! – and, second, what could be termed a 'mystery' element, which can really fascinate students, drive them on and engage them.

The value of using games, quizzes and puzzles as an occasional activity should certainly not be underestimated. One tutor told me, for instance, that he set a puzzle for students in every class he led, introducing it at the start of a class and revealing the answer at the end.

Another tutor explained his special Christmas group session in which he would take out all 15 library copies of a famous biography and ask students questions about the book. The students, with copies of the book in front of them, would then have to discover the answers. This tactic not only introduced variety but also forced students into broadening their knowledge. Thus, puzzles can provoke and inspire students, and direct them towards further, perhaps more orthodox, study.

I would like to thank Martin Davies, Philip Woodfine, Derek Lynch and Bill Roberts for supplying ideas for this chapter.

Related activities

The following activities, outlined and explained in other chapters, also include an important 'game' element:

8

Trivia quiz

In a nutshell

This makes a good winding-down activity for finishing a course, with all the questions linked to topics on the syllabus.

Aims

1. To refresh and recap on key facts and events which are often ignored amid the analytical emphasis of academic courses.
2. To provoke teamwork and the desire to know!

What is needed

- Quiz questions, prepared by the teacher or a group of students.
- Answer sheets

Time required

20 minutes (quiz) plus 10 minutes (answers) plus 10 minutes (plenary – to discuss issues raised by the quiz).

How it works

Students are asked to form teams of equal size and the tutor asks the questions. The answers are read out, and is followed by the post-quiz discussion.

A good example in action: Psychology – main themes in modern psychology

QUESTIONS

1. Who are generally regarded as the father figures of American psychology?
2. Which law did E.L. Thorndike devise?
3. What was More's 'degeneration hypothesis'?
4. When did Darwin publish *The Descent of Man*?
5. What did Papez's famous paper of 1931 propose?

ANSWERS

1. William James and G. Stanley Hall.
2. The 'law of effect'.
3. Degenerations are deviations from the normal human type which are transmissible by heredity and which deteriorate progressively towards extinction.
4. 1871.
5. A neurological mechanism for emotion.

Advantages of this activity

1. It stimulates team rivalry.
2. It emphasizes the need for detail and accuracy.

Potential problem

Quizzes may be perceived by students as a cop-out: they may consider quizzes to have no educational value and consequently might not attend.

Main learning outcome

Students will learn that accuracy and detail are important, not only in quizzes, but in essays too!

Variation

One group of students can be asked to set a course quiz for another.

9

Card games

In a nutshell

Card games can be an excellent test of students' intellectual dexterity. Give them an array of cards to link, relate and generally manipulate.

Aims

1. To bring ideas, events, people and organizations alive via the use of specially designed cards.
2. To encourage students to see links and relationships between different phcnomena.

What is needed

A set of 'cards', pre-prepared by either the tutor or a small student group (before or during the class).

Time required

10 minutes (small-group discussion) plus 15 minutes (whole-group discussion).

How it works

The tutor – or even a small group of students – takes 30 index cards. On each is written an idea, an event, a person or an organization (roughly the same number of

31

each), all of which have featured in the set course or in the study of a particular topic. Small student subgroups are handed a mixed handful of cards and each is asked to point out the nature and extent of relationships, or non-relationships, between the words and terms written on their cards. This can provoke good, incisive discussion and, because the cards are 'real' and 'visible', students can manoeuvre them physically.

Each group nominates a spokesperson who reveals the 'links' to the tutor and the whole group. Discussion can then continue, primarily on the nature of the relationships between the ideas, events, people and organizations that featured on the cards. There might also be debate about the difficulties inherent in the exercise and the main points to emerge from it.

A good example in action: Philosophy – Marxism

A group might be given the following cards:

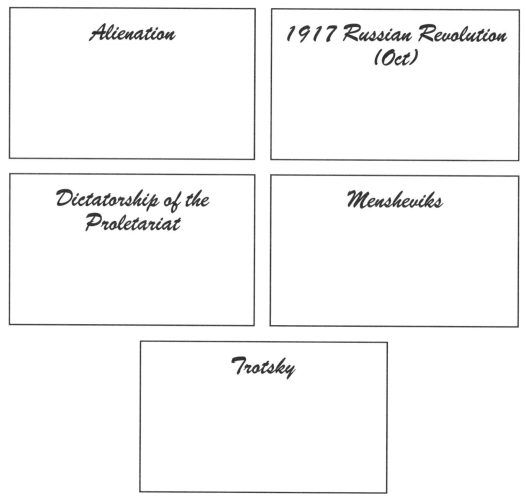

What are the exact relationships and, perhaps more importantly, the non-relationships between the five terms?

Advantages of this activity

1. It encourages students to think about the nature of relationships between variables.
2. It can provoke very healthy small-group discussion.
3. Externalizing ideas and other variables onto pieces of card can make them more accessible and malleable.

Potential problem

Students may try to contrive relationships where there are none – it should be emphasized that pointing out total 'non-links' is as valid as discerning clear and definite relationships.

Main learning outcome

Students will have gained a valuable insight into the diverse types of relationship that link ideas, people, events and organizations.

Variation

Instead of giving students a mix of cards, give them a set of 'ideas' only (or 'events' or 'personalities' or 'organizations' only) and ask them to do the same exercise – discerning in what sense the cards are linked or relate to each other.

10

The end-of-term opinion poll

In a nutshell

During the last week of a course, why not round off proceedings with a student 'opinion poll', with all questions relating to the content of the course, and with students voting on all the main issues and controversies? The results can then be used as a stimulus to further discussion and debate – a nice conclusion to a course!

Aims

1. To create an interesting and stimulating end to a course.
2. To investigate a set of underlying and intriguing core questions that might otherwise be slightly neglected during the usually frenetic end-of-term period.

What is needed

● A set of opinion poll questions, devised either by the tutor or a small group of students.
● An OHP and blank OHP slides on which to record the poll results.

Time required

20 minutes (to answer the poll questions), plus 10 minutes (to collate results), plus 20 minutes (to discuss poll results).

How it works

The tutor hands out the poll forms to student pairs at the beginning of the class. The students deliberate on their answers – the poll questions can be a real stimulus to focused discussion – and, after 20 minutes, the tutor collates the results of the poll on the OHP at the front of the class.

With the key student verdicts displayed on the OHP, the class can be divided into small buzz groups to discuss the meaning of the results. What are the main surprises? Were the results predictable? What were the problems with the poll questions and the general opinion poll process?

A good example in action: History – British imperialism

SAMPLE QUESTION

Q1. How would you rank Britain's real imperial motives in the late nineteenth century? (Rank 1–5: 5 = most important motive.)

- Economic   —
- Political   —
- Security-based   —
- Spreading civilization'   —
- 'Racial superiority'   —

Class totals:

- Economic   87
- Political   56
- Security-based   24
- 'Spreading civilization'   26
- 'Racial superiority'   69

These final figures could then be used as an excellent discussion-provoker. Where do economic and political motives merge? Was spreading civilization just an 'excuse'? What were Britain's precise economic motivations?

Advantages of this activity

1. It crystallizes key issues and controversies.
2. It attempts to quantify student opinion.
3. The poll results can act as a very spontaneous spur to discussion and debate.

Potential problem

Many nuanced academic questions are, obviously, very difficult to simplify into one-line poll questions, but it can be quite interesting to try, and good discussion can follow.

Main learning outcome

Students will be able to weigh up their own opinions on key questions and debate them with other class members.

11

Geography puzzles

In a nutshell

Maps are a key accessory to many college courses. Why not make maps central to study by creating games out of them?

Aims

1. To emphasize the geographical dimension to topics.
2. To foster competition and rivalry for the benefit of individual students and class discussion as a whole.

What is needed

Copies of relevant map(s).

Time required

15 minutes (small-group discussion of maps) plus 10 minutes (feedback session).

How it works

Copies of the key map are distributed to students. They are asked to add to the map in graphic or diagrammatic form – perhaps representing or depicting key developments, events, movements or trends. The students can be asked to do this on the spot – as a surprise when they walk into the class – or prior to the group session (thus allowing them to exploit library facilities).

In the class the students can talk through their thoughts in small groups – comparing and contrasting where they have drawn lines or arrows. The tutor can then tie things up, and attempt to reach some conclusions, by revealing the real answers and chairing a whole-group discussion.

A good example in action: Politics – regions in international rela tions

I've got a geography game. I lecture on world regions, and one important aspect of this topic is the subjectivity of these regions. For example, the terms Eastern Europe and Central Europe have very different connotations. Germany and Austria, for instance, would not enjoy the backward connotations that go with the Eastern Europe term.

The game that I play with my students relates to this. Asia, for example, is unknown. Instead of giving the students reading on this subject I tell them to look at atlases – to go to Geography in the library rather than Politics. The exercise is to locate boundaries and regions within Asia – for example, East Asia, South Asia and so on. Where are the boundaries? Where are the ethnic and racial groups?

I gave a blank map of Asia out at the end of one seminar, and then at the next one I went round the group, asking each person in turn for their answers, and we emerged with some common answers. We then discussed boundaries. There were some right answers and there was some consensus; there were, if you like, approximate answers. The key question was this: why draw lines where they are? What are the criteria for deciding on regions like the Pacific Rim – social, economic, cultural, linguistic or strategic? All in all, it's probably more of a quiz than a game.
Dr Derek Lynch, Lecturer in Politics, University of Huddersfield

WHERE ARE THE 'REGIONS'?

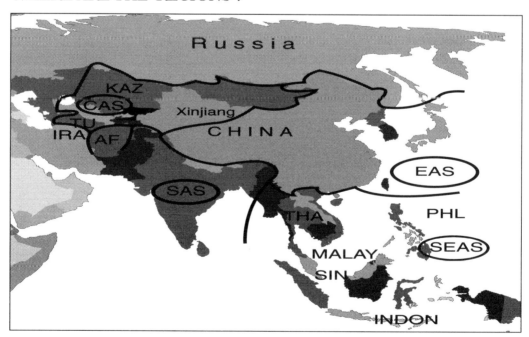

Possible answers:

- CAS – Central Asia
- SAS – South Asia
- EAS – East Asia
- SEAS – South-east Asia.

Advantages of this activity

1. It contributes a sizeable, refreshing visual element to a topic.
2. Students' ideas and points do not have to be expressed through words, but can be made via lines or arrows drawn on a map.

Potential problems

Students may have a natural reluctance to be artistic or creative – even when it's just a case of drawing arrows! Also, they may expect that there are right answers – there usually aren't!

Main learning outcome

Students will become highly sensitive to the significance of geography and to the way in which ideas and arguments can be represented in graphic form.

12

The most reasons

In a nutshell

Inject a healthy dose of competition into groupwork sessions! Ask small student sub-groups to write down as many argument points as they can ('factors', 'reasons', 'causes', 'consequences' or whatever) to help the class explore a crucial issue or debate.

Aims

1. To stimulate interest in a topic.
2. To encourage diversity and originality in thinking.

What is needed

● A3 paper.
● Blu-tack.
● Felt-tip marker pens.

Time required

10 minutes (in small groups) plus 15 minutes (whole-group discussion).

How it works

The tutor introduces the important issue for group debate. It might involve the consideration of 'reasons for', 'factors causing' or 'consequences of' some aspect of the topic. The class is split up into smaller groups, and each group is asked to think of as many relevant points as possible. These are then listed by the students in poster form.

The tutor then chairs a plenary session in which he or she – or another student subgroup (which could be acting as 'referee') – awards marks or points for the quality of each item on the poster lists in terms of relevance, importance, plausibility and so on.

Extra 'points' can be acquired for original or impressively argued points, since discussion is intrinsic to all stages of this exercise. The winner is eventually announced!

A good example in action: Economics – unemployment

What are the main causes of unemployment?

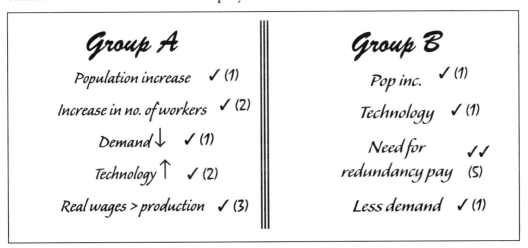

Note: Marks awarded by the 'referee' are shown in brackets.

Advantages of this activity

1. It adds an urgent, competitive element.
2. It promotes teamwork.
3. It has a high analytical content.
4. Focused discussion in small groups is encouraged.

Potential problem

Where does one point begin and another end? Students may be more concerned with winning than understanding!

Main learning outcome

Students will be forced to diversify their answers and to think beyond the predictable factors.

Revision games

Revision can be made far more interesting through the use of games. The following activities (13–19) are 'revision only' strategies: they are quick, good fun and they all have some educational merit!

They aim to make a traditionally boring part of students' life – revision – slightly more enjoyable. They should also stimulate students and promote more interest in key subjects and topics.

13

The name game*

How it works

The tutor asks each student to write down, on a piece of paper, the name of a key personality, an important idea or doctrine to emerge from the course, a significant event or development or a well-known academic theory or thesis.

Students then fold up their bits of paper and throw them in a tub or hat. The class divides into two teams. Team A begins and their lead-off person pulls out a piece of paper and has to describe or explain the person/idea/event to the other members of his team without using clues such as rhyming words.

Each individual has one minute to get through as many pieces of paper as he or she can – with team members shouting out the answer as soon as they know what or who is being described or explained. The game then passes to the other team. The winning side is the one which identifies most terms.

A good example in action: RE – religious leaders and terms

Names and terms to explain:

- John Wesley
- Mormonism
- Ayotollah Khomeini
- Purgatory
- Kingdom of God
- Mecca.

How would students describe and explain these names and terms?

*Adapted from BBC TV's *They Think It's All Over!*

Advantages of this activity

1. It is extremely good fun.
2. Students have to be particularly clever in the way that they try to explain their terms.
3. It requires a good breadth of knowledge.
4. It promotes healthy team rivalry and involvement.

Potential problem

Students might, unknowingly, duplicate the items they write on their pieces of paper, so advise them to select fairly original names and terms.

14

Blockbusters*

How it works

The tutor – or a selected group of students – creates an OHP Blockbusters-style panel for two teams of students to compete on. The panel should comprise a 'big' square full of 'little' squares, with each little square containing the initial letter(s) of a word, phrase, idea, name or term that featured in the course.

The aim of the game is for the two sides to move across the board as quickly as possible, from left to right (or vice versa) by answering questions on the letters on which they land during their journey. If a team answers correctly, it is entitled to another question and can choose another adjacent square to move to. A team's progress across the panel can be indicated by a counter (a button, for example). The 'question's should cover all aspects of a course and should generally take the form of cryptic clues.

A good example in action: Geography – key terms

The following are examples of the letters that might be written on some of the small squares followed by the clue-type question and answer.

- CHHR – hypothetical scheme which attempts to explain the location of cities (Christaller's Hexagonal Hierarchy of Regions)
- TUHIEAW – crucial academic study which defines and classifies towns by their functions (The Urban Hierarchy in England and Wales)
- U – the long-term process resulting in growth of towns and cities (Urbanization)
- BDCE – theory concerning the social pattern of the Western city (Burgess's Diagram of City Ecology)

*Adapted from the ITV programme of the same name.

● CBD – the focus for skyscraper development in large conurbations (Central Business District)

Advantages of this activity

1. It is good for memory-jogging.
2. It is grossly competitive!

Potential problem

Considerable preparation is involved – the tutor needs to create a rather intricate panel or board for the game to take place.

15

Party quirks*

How it works

One student acts out the role of a party host, welcoming 'guests' (in turn) to his or her gathering. Other students are each allocated a personality or figure from the course they are studying (the tutor can create a guest list prior to the class and the 'guests' can choose their own identity). The rest of the group act as the audience.

The host, naturally, does not know the identity of his or her guests. Only the host can initiate a conversation and direct his or her questions towards uncovering the guests' identities. The guests role-play their identities; they can talk; but can only respond to questions with the words 'Yes' or 'No'.

A good example in action: Psychology – modern thinkers

The following people, exhibiting exaggerated behaviour, arrive at the party...

- Freud (overtly sexual, observing everyone for their class, their sexual characteristics and sexuality, and looking in odd places).
- Spock (one-dimensional in his conversation-starters. For example, 'Have you got children?'; 'How do you treat them?'; 'How are they growing up?' and so on).
- Pavlov (assessing behaviour, looking for dogs and constantly experimenting with the guests).
- Cattle (asking questions, looking for patterns of behaviour and developing personality profiles for all guests).
- Allport (analysing all the guests for their personality traits and characteristics, and what they have in common).

*Adapted from Channel 4's *Whose Line Is It Anyway?*

What observations do the audience make? Is it easy to guess who is who? If not, why not? How are the key figures different? What do they have in common? How would they get on? Who would be talking to whom?

Advantages of this activity

1. It's extremely good fun!
2. If the 'guests' have to get into their character and empathize, they will be forced to think and learn from their experience.
3. The host has to ask intelligent questions and deduce identities from sparse information. He or she will have to show impressive knowledge and awareness of the course's detail and scope.

Potential problem

Care needs to be taken that the characters to be played are not only as varied and unusual as possible, but also guessable.

16

The alphabet

How it works

This is a good quick exercise. The tutor allocates each student a couple of different letters so as to cover all 26 letters of the alphabet. For each of the letters they have been given, the students are asked to think of an issue, theory, personality or event from the course. They then write these topics down on pieces of paper and throw them into a container. The tutor takes the pieces of paper out of the container. To the first student sitting on his or her left he or she reads out the 'A' topic, to the second student on his or her left the 'B' item and so on.

Each student under the spotlight has to introduce, define, and elaborate upon his or her subject for a couple of minutes, with the tutor and the other students then engaging in relevant discussion.

A good example in action: English – literary terms

- **Student 1**: *Alliteration* – 'The repetition of the same consonant or vowel at the beginning of words in a sequence. For example, "He was mean, moody, and magnificent".'
- **Student 2**: *Bathos* – 'Intentional anticlimax or deflation. Used by writers to move from the serious and elevated to the trivial and lowly for comic or satiric effect. For example, "What female heart can gold despise?"; "What cat's averse to fish?" (from Gray's *Ode to the Death of a Favourite Cat*).
- **Student 3**: *Cliché* – 'Signifies an expression which deviates enough from ordinary usage to call attention to itself and has been used so often that it is felt to be hackneyed or cloying. For example, "I'm as sick as a parrot".'
- **Student 4**: *Doggerel* – 'A term applied to rough, heavy-footed and jerky poetry, usually the result of ineptitude on the part of the poet, but occasionally employed deliberately for comic effect. For example, "Roses are red, Violets are blue, I think you're great, But you don't appear to like me too much".'

● **Student 5**: *Euphemism* – 'The use of a vaguer, more roundabout term in place of a term that is considered blunt, disagreeable or offensive. For example, "She has passed on", instead of "She is dead".'

Advantages of this activity

1. It involves everyone.
2. It covers valuable ground – a maximum of 26 key topic areas!
3. Productive discussion can easily be stimulated.

Potential problem

Make sure that the students write down realistic and feasible topic areas. Another problem may be finding suitable topics for the letters 'X', 'Q' and 'Z'.

17

Top 5

How it works

This is a very simple activity. At the end of a course, students are asked to rank a range of different items – for example, 'the top five intellectuals covered in the syllabus', 'the top five concepts covered on the course, ranked by importance', 'the top five events or economic/political developments that took place during the era' – the possibilities are endless!

Students then devise their 'Top 5' lists in pairs or small groups. The lists can be written in felt-tip pen and then pinned to the wall to show the range of student choice and opinion. A whole-group discussion then follows.

A good example in action: Sociology – functionalism

Who are the 'Top 5' functionalists?

STUDENT LIST

- Comte
- Spencer
- Durkheim
- Parsons
- Merton.

DISCUSSION

Why are these people viewed as the most important functionalists? What was their most significant contribution? Who is the most important?

Advantages of this activity

1. It forces students to be selective and to prioritize effectively.
2. Students have to justify their selections, which will make them think about the reasons for their choice and their general rationale.
3. It generates a spontaneous and wide-ranging discussion.

Potential problem

It is obviously an oversimplification of the topic to isolate distinct ideas and events, let alone try to rank their importance.

18

Martians

How it works

Students, in turn, act the part of a Martian who has recently landed on Earth. The other students, in turn, are given a set of cards, each denoting a different concept, theory or idea.

Given that the Martian knows nothing at all about Earth, its history and its traditions, the individual students have to explain, in very basic terms, the concepts or terms written on the cards. The skill here is for students to return to first principles and impress the Martian with their simple, clear expositions of difficult terms.

A good example in action: Philosophy – Explain the term *liberty*

Student: 'Liberty is an abstract idea.'
Martian: 'What is an abstract idea?'
Student: 'An abstract idea is something that cannot be seen or touched – a concept that exists in one's mind.'
Martian: 'Mind?'
Student: 'In one's mental zone. It's where you think.'

And so on . . .

Advantages of this activity

1. It is extremely challenging, and only the committed, effective and enthusiastic explainers will succeed.
2. Explaining key ideas and concepts from first principles is an admirable academic skill.

3.   It will provoke discussion among all the students as to how best to articulate a key idea and as to what are the most fundamental features of a concept.

Potential problem

The Martian could understand things too easily and quickly! He or she must remember to play dumb, but must also try to be logical!

19

Just a minute

How it works

Students write down a topic or issue on a piece of paper. All the pieces of paper are thrown into a suitable receptacle, and each student then picks out one. With the tutor or a student monitoring a stopwatch, each student has to speak continuously on their topic for one or two minutes. Other students 'beep' and interject when the speaker is veering away from the subject, hesitating, waffling, or becoming irrelevant.

A good example in action: Law – key concepts

Students are asked to talk for one minute on the following topics:

- criminal defamatory libel
- blasphemy
- sedition
- obscenity
- malicious falsehoods.

What did the student talkers learn from this experience? On each topic, which main issues were covered? What did the listeners learn?

Advantages of this activity

1. It focuses students' minds!
2. Students have to use their memories, not only to dredge up information, but also for more overtly academic skills – for example, they have to consider such

questions as 'How can I elaborate more on this?', 'How can I develop this point?', 'What does this idea link into?'

3. It has a very challenging format.
4. The process forces students to prioritize and ask themselves: 'What are the really important points, ideas and arguments I need to get across, before people start interrupting me?'

Potential problem

The topics need to be challenging, but neither too straightforward nor too obscure.

Summary and evaluation

Games as teaching activities are often mocked and ridiculed: 'Surely you can't do that?!'

The weight of opinion, however, is that games and puzzles can be of great educational value. Whether the games in question are quizzes, opinion polls or specially designed board games, the feeling is that students can be stimulated and enthused by what, on the surface, might appear as rather shallow and superficial games. Games can bring competition, rivalry and fun – three very underestimated qualities. They can create an incomparable buzz and can start pulses racing.

But, somehow, games and puzzles have a credibility problem. They are often viewed as simplistic and crude – and not the kind of tool that 'sophisticated' academics should be embracing. Enlightened observers, however, know that games can work: they can relax and invigorate students as well as encourage them to delve deeper into a subject. Above all, games, quizzes and puzzles can be good, harmless fun and can enliven the most dreary of subjects.

Clearly, reading, essay-writing and preparation for classroom sessions are serious tasks that require determination and hard work, and these elements cannot be bypassed. But games can add a priceless ingredient to classes. They can inject entertainment and enjoyment, and act as a springboard to further study.

3 Worksheets

The students actually enjoy working with each other and working together. You can often hear them explaining things to their friends in their own terms; they like showing each other how to do things and how to solve problems.
Chris Barton, Senior Lecturer in Economics, University of Huddersfield

Introduction

With the heavy emphasis on oral discussion and debate, group sessions are often devoid of a written element. It is, however, possible to change this state of affairs, to rectify it, and to introduce a problem-solving, worksheet, element into class sessions. Here the use of study sheets, tests and questionnaires, among other things, can provoke discussion and aid students' efforts to understand and clarify important issues. Such study aids can also give students something concrete to take home with them for further use and for revision.

In this chapter, therefore, a series of practical ideas on the worksheet theme are introduced, outlined and explored. As group activities they all have one factor in common – an overtly student-friendly rationale. In addition, the documentation that accompanies each strategy can include blank spaces and boxes, in which students can be encouraged to insert their own thoughts and ideas on set issues in written, diagrammatic or graphic form.

I would like to thank Andrew Taylor, Chris Barton and Jill Leckey for their help with this chapter.

Related activities

The following activities, outlined and explained in other chapters, also include an important 'worksheet' element:

20

The workbook

In a nutshell

Students work through a pre-prepared 'workbook'. The workbook can incorporate a variety of exercises: tables to complete, blank boxes to fill in with definitions and summaries, graphs and diagrams to analyse, true-or-false puzzles to grapple with and multiple-choice questions to answer.

Aims

1. To stimulate students through small-scale, but highly challenging, written tasks.
2. To work through an array of different exercises, and thus to use group sessions as an arena for practical, problem-solving work.
3. To encourage students to help other students with the activities involved.

What is needed

A pre-prepared and mass-produced workbook – to run parallel to the course syllabus and to incorporate a range of tasks.

Time required

Whole sessions can be devoted to workbook activity, but perhaps the tutor does need to vary the format of such classes to include phases of pairwork, small-group work and tutor-led discussion.

How it works

Workbooks can be used intermittently or set courses can be structured around workbook use. Students can work through them in pairs or small groups and the tutor can circulate. Workbook exercises can also be used on a more occasional basis – allocated, for example, to 15- or 20-minute slots in selected classes.

A good example in action: Sociology – society

1. What Is Society?

That sociologists study 'society' is self evident and yet 'society' is itself a slippery concept; we use it often in everyday speech but rarely think very much about what it actually means when we say such things as, 'society doesn't care anymore' or 'society is to blame for poverty or crime'. Mrs Thatcher once, famously said, 'There is no such thing as society; there are only individual men and women and their families'. This exercise is designed as a first step in helping you think through the concept of society and arrive at your own conclusions.

Step 1
Each person in the group should write down on a piece of paper their own definition of society. These should then be folded over and placed in a container. (Not assessed)

Your own original definition of society. *(Not assessed)*
26 Words

Step 2
Take each definition out in turn and read it out to the group. Assess each definition in terms of its positive and negative features. Try to identify the different dimensions of the concept on which the different definitions are based.

Step 3
Try to arrive at a group definition that incorporates what you see as the essential features of a good definition. (Not assessed)

Write here the group definition of society. *(Not assessed)*
50 Words

Source: Division of Sociology, University of Huddersfield.

Advantages of this activity

1. Students know 'where they are' – they can work through tasks at their own speed.
2. In the small-group context, students do tend to enjoy helping other students in problem-solving tasks, explaining a problem they have mastered and helping other students understand it
3. If necessary, the tutor can spend most of his or her time with the less able class members.

Potential problem

The workbooks need a great deal of pre-preparation and planning.

Main learning outcome

Students will be stimulated, and enabled to learn by a set of well planned and focused exercises.

21

Themes

In a nutshell

This tactic is designed to draw out key themes across a course. Students are asked to deliberate on, and then fill in, 'study cards' produced by the tutor – cards which can ultimately provoke good and highly relevant student discussion.

Aims

1. To focus students' attention on key continuities and themes evident within a course.
2. To force students to think in a different way – that is, to consider global themes rather than questions on specific syllabus topics.

What is needed

● Pre-prepared study cards.

Time required

15 minutes (small-group discussion and filling-in of the study cards) plus 10 minutes (whole-group discussion based on student answers).

How it works

The tutor hands out identical copies of a set study card to small student groups (pairs or threes). Each study card includes its own instructions. Students have to complete the card and, in the process, they will be able to discuss key issues and record their group's views on it. The tutor then chairs a whole-group discussion on the key points to emerge from the exercise. At the end of the class, copies are made of each card and distributed to all group members, so that students can benefit from the work of their colleagues. Later, the cards can be used to recap on key themes and also utilized as a key revision aid.

A good example in action: History of Ideas – the French Far Right

<u>Plots, conspiracies and *coup d'états* on the Extreme Right (1871 to the Present Day): Success or failure?</u>

1889	Boulanger	Embryonic and aborted?
1899	Déroulède and the Anti-Dreyfusards	A farce and a fiasco?
1934	Fascist *ligues*, 6 February	More an anti-parliamentary riot?
1958	Army rebels in Algeria	Counter-productive – de Gaulle?

<u>Questions</u>

1. Do you agree with the *coup* 'verdicts' on the right-hand side of the table?

2. Would you add any other *coups* to the table?

3. What are the exact aims of the four *coups* detailed above?

4. Why is the extreme right, in all its various forms, so bad at seizing power? Or is it?

Source: Division of History, University of Huddersfield.

Advantages of this activity

1. It encourages very focused thematic thinking.
2. Students are able to air their initial ideas in the confidence-boosting atmosphere of small-group work.
3. The cards can build up into a 'set' – ideal for revision purposes.

Potential problem

Because students have to write down their answers on a study card, they may start to think that there are 'definite' or 'correct' answers, but this, clearly, may not be the case! Discussion is the name of the game!

Main learning outcome

Students will engage in discussion and in-depth analysis of a key theme or issue – and they will have a well structured card to refer back to and to use for revision.

22

Multiple choice

In a nutshell

This is a commonly utilized strategy – but not in humanities and social science classes. Nevertheless, multiple-choice exercises have much to recommend them.

Aims

1. To simplify key issues and debates.
2. To stimulate debate – but also to offer definite answers.
3. To engender learning through small-group discussion – and through making mistakes.

What is needed

Multiple-choice tests, to be produced by either the tutor or students.

Time required

15 minutes (small-group work on the multiple-choice tests) plus 15 minutes (revelation of answers followed by a discussion chaired by the tutor).

How it works

The tutor, or a group of students, devises a simple multiple-choice test. Each individual question comes with a set of optional 'answers' of which one (or more) will be correct. In pairs or small groups students discuss their responses and complete their question sheets. The tutor reveals the answers and leads a focused discussion on each one.

A good example in action: Economics – elasticity

ELASTICITY

1. Income elasticity of demand for a commodity measures the responsiveness of

    A   price to changes in income.
    B   income to changes in price.
    C   quantity demanded to changes in income.
    D   quantity demanded to changes in price.

2. If the demand for a product is relatively price inelastic, the effect of an increase in price on the quantity sold and on consumer expenditure on that product would be that

    A   both quantity and expenditure would rise.
    B   quantity would fall but expenditure would rise.
    C   quantity would rise but expenditure would fall.
    D   both quantity and expenditure would fall.

3. Income elasticity of demand for a good will be zero when demand for the commodity

    A   rises by a larger proportion than the increase in income.
    B   does not change with an increase in income.
    C   falls with an increase in income.
    D   rises by a smaller proportion than the increase in income.
    E   rises by the same proportion as the increase in income.

4. A firm is considering increasing its price from £1 to £1.10. From previous experience it knows its price elasticity of demand is (–) 1.5. The quantity it sells at present is 12,000 units. What will be the quantity the firm will expect to sell if it increases its price to £1.10, assuming that all other things remain the same?

    A   10,200
    B   10,500
    C   10,800
    D   11,200
    E   13,200

5. At a price of £4, an industry supplies 30 units of output per week. If the elasticity of supply between the prices of £4 and £5 per unit is 2, how many units will be supplied at £5?

    A   60
    B   45
    C   42
    D   15

Source: Division of Economics, University of Huddersfield.

Advantages of this activity

1. It simplifies complex issues.
2. It catalyses small-group discussion.
3. The right answer is there to be identified – and this will add a real impetus to discussion.

Potential problem

Some subjects and topics are very difficult to simplify into multiple-choice questions and answers and this technique may, therefore, have its limitations.

Main learning outcomes

Students will be involved in a short and incisive problem-solving exercise, and will gain in confidence from identifying, and then arguing around, correct answers.

Variation

The multiple-choice approach may be particularly valuable when the subject matter is an abstract idea or theory. By being able to see arguments and ideas written down, and then having to choose between set options, students will improve their ability to conceptualize.

23

Role-play questionnaires

In a nutshell

This activity adds a new and highly productive dimension to role-play by asking students 'in character' to answer a structured questionnaire about the nature, beliefs and motivations of their personality.

Aims

1.   To give a little more structure and analytical clarity to role-play sessions.
2.   To help students empathize with their character more, and to provoke discussion about the role-play.

What is needed

Questionnaires pre-prepared by the tutor.

Time required

15 minutes (questionnaires) plus 15 minutes (plenary discussion).

How it works

Students, in pairs or groups of three, are allocated a role-play character (student groups could get the same character or different ones depending on the situation). Each group is given a questionnaire to be completed in line with the mindset of

69

their allocated character. Good focused discussion ensues while the questionnaire is being filled in, and then the tutor chairs a plenary session on all the responses given.

A good example in action: English – *Hamlet* questionnaire

Each student group is asked to empathize with the character, Hamlet, and answer the following questions:

1. How do you feel about your new stepfather, the King?
2. Are you pleased your mother has remarried?
3. Who do you feel that you can trust?
4. How do you think that Denmark should be ruled?
5. What are your feelings for Ophelia?
6. How do you feel about your father's death?
7. How do you see your future?
8. Who and what do you fear?

Advantages of this activity

1. It generates creative small-group discussion.
2. As role-play characters, students have to pin down focused answers to definite questions.
3. Tensions, rivalries and contrasts between the set players in the role-play will emerge in the plenary discussion, when responses are revealed orally.

Potential problem

The questionnaire needs to be designed so that it applies to all role-play characters and players equally.

Main learning outcome

Through thinking 'in character' and completing the questionnaires, students will acquire awareness of the various perspectives on the central issue, and debate will be stimulated around these different views.

It is not a 'worksheet' as such, but ...dent subgroup picking, and then ...ds.

...planned and carefully devised ques-

...small-group ideas and thoughts in

What is needed

- Index cards (pre-printed with questions).
- Pens.

Time required

10 minutes (small-group work on the 'card questions') plus 15 minutes (whole-group plenary discussion).

How it works

The tutor writes a selection of provocative questions on separate index cards. The cards are thrown into a hat or other container and each student subgroup picks out one card. The questions on the card set the agenda for the various small-group discussions, and the spokesperson for each mini-group notes down the key ideas and arguments aired in the 10-minute sessions.

All groups must make an effort to fill their cards with relevant ideas and thoughts about the question. Each group can then either reveal its thoughts on its assigned question or the cards can be returned to the hat or container, and each group can be asked to pick out another group's card and interpret the ideas and arguments put forward on the card that they select.

A good example in action: Geography – urbanization

Individual student mini-groups might receive the following questions to discuss:

What is a town?	*What was the nature of pre-industrial cities?*
What factors affect the process of urbanization?	*How should cities be classified?*

Advantages of this activity

1.   There is a nice element of suspense in terms of anticipating the difficulty of the question.
2.   The blank space on the cards has quite a powerful message: it must be filled up with good, original ideas!
3.   The card gives a visible focus to the small-group discussions.

Potential problem

The usual with small-group work: the occasional dominating student, the drift of conversation on to irrelevant topics and so on.

Main learning outcome

Students will be engaged in the cut-and-thrust of question-answering, discussion, and perhaps even question-asking.

Variation

Instead of the tutor writing the questions on the cards, the students could be asked to formulate the questions themselves, and write them on the cards. The activity could then proceed on the basis of each subgroup answering another subgroup's question.

Summary and evaluation

Worksheets, study cards and answer sheets are perhaps an underused type of classroom activity, perhaps because the prevailing notion is that classroom sessions are about verbalization and oral discussion, and not about biros, writing and the filling-in of blank boxes. To go along with this view, however, would be to limit the potential and possibilities of small group work.

First, it is clear that students value, and enjoy, having a written record of classroom endeavours. A proportion of students do actually try to take notes during normal group sessions, often against the tutor's wishes and, most probably, with fairly indifferent results. Organized, structured and student-friendly worksheet-style exercises could have many benefits – one of which might well be an end to the unhealthy practice of students trying to scribble notes when the tutor wants their full attention on the discussion at hand. In this sense, the regular use of written exercises might have advantages for both students and staff.

Second, a worksheet formula can also give groupwork sessions a ready-made framework and structure: 'Let's work through the following questions over the next hour…' Furthermore, direct written questions and the need for concise and cogent responses compel students to focus incisively on the issue. While a whole-group discussion can veer off the subject, and can easily lose its cutting edge, an ordered written or graphic exercise has the potential to be relevant, clearly targeted and highly stimulating. We need to remember, too, that small-group discussion will, necessarily, accompany the written efforts of all individual students, pairs and small groups when confronted by questions, graphs, diagrams or blank boxes to fill in.

With worksheets, however, the disadvantage is the substantial pre-preparation required of the tutor. Workbooks and study cards need detailed planning, serious forethought and a generous photocopying budget. However, if tutors can seize the initiative, the benefits may be fulsome: smart designer workbooks, ready-made classroom stimuli and a rolling programme of ordered and focused group discussion.

4　Groupwork

My feeling is that small groups shouldn't just talk. I think there should be activity – to go alongside the conversation.
Rev. Sue Havens, Anglican Chaplain, University of Manchester

Introduction

Most experts agree that real, constructive discussion can only genuinely take place in small groups. While some productive activities can take place in the whole-group context, it is often a healthy idea to create subgroups – from the simple pair, through threesomes and foursomes, up to larger groups of five, six or seven. The rationale here is that students often need the privacy of small groups and the company of their peers before they feel ready to open up, discuss and argue.

Once the tutor has created a set of subgroups there are many options. The small student groups can have a constant, 'trusting' membership over several weeks or a whole term, or their make-up can be 'randomized'; they can work on the same task as 'syndicates', or on different tasks; they can just 'buzz' or they can be asked to 'do' or 'produce' something; they can stay intact for a whole class or they can be asked to merge, to form bigger groups. Groupwork has huge potential.

It should be noted that, even though this chapter is devoted to specific and quite distinct groupwork activities, *all* the other strategies explained in this book revolve fundamentally around groupwork – usually relying on the formation of subgroups, but at times also employing whole-group formats.

I would like to thank the following people for their ideas on groupwork: Allen Warren, Martin Davies, Inderjit Bhogal and Marilyn Pursglove. Where I have expanded upon other people's techniques – or when my ideas have coincided or overlapped with published ideas – I have quoted the relevant source and reference in full.

Related activities

All the activities contained in this book are, to some extent, based on groupwork and its different forms.

25

The committee system

In a nutshell

This system increases student involvement and 'ownership', but also leaves room for an authoritative tutor input.

Aims

1. To involve students in the organization and running of a group session.
2. To incorporate student opinion and staff expertise.

What is needed

A general topic for discussion!

Time required

Two hours.

How it works

The tutor begins the session with a ten-minute introduction – notices, background information, general context-setting – but then leaves the room for 30 minutes. In this time, the students, acting as a 'committee', have to organize an agenda and schedule for the group and allocate key roles: chair, presenter, discussant and any other set roles that are required.

The tutor returns, and acts as an ordinary group member for the following hour – inputting where appropriate (pointing out technical points, factual errors and so on), but generally keeping a fairly low profile. The class ends with a 20-minute summary or commentary from the tutor, analysing the discussion, its merits and its defects.

A good example in action: Law – slander and defamation

1. **Introduction**. The tutor introduces the general topic and chairs a brief discussion aimed at defining the two central terms (15 minutes).
2. **Committee stage**. The tutor leaves the room, and the student 'committee' sets the class agenda. What are the main controversies surrounding slander and defamation? What are the main issues and debates? (30 minutes).
3. **Discussion**. The students lead class discussion and the tutor sits in (60 minutes). Questions to be discussed might be:

    ●   What is the difference between slander and defamation?
    ●   Significant cases: what issues do they raise?
    ●   What are the problems inherent in the two terms?

4. **Conclusion**. The tutor summarizes and comments on the discussion (15 minutes).

Advantages of this activity

1. The activity involves a balanced mix of student and staff input.
2. The students are responsible for their group session and their learning.
3. The tutor's non-presence, and then presence, can affect the dynamics and atmosphere of the class in a very positive way.

Potential problem

The students might not feel confident about the topic, nor about the idea of scheduling the class themselves. The tutor must emphasize that he or she is not looking for a perfect class, but merely for an enthusiastic performance.

Main learning outcome

Students will produce their own class session, and will benefit from both their own input and that of the tutor.

26

Pairwork and buzz groups

In a nutshell

Splitting students into small subgroups is a standard strategy and, on a whole range of fronts, a good and healthy idea. Here is one particular groupwork idea: split the class up into twos, threes, fours or fives and let them loose on a particular task – studying a document (a small text, cartoon or poster perhaps) or maybe just considering 'factors' or 'reasons' that link into, or underlie, the main discussion topic.

Aims

1. To give students confidence – in the 'safe' context of pairwork.
2. To break up the monotony of whole-group work.
3. To get the pairs working on specific tasks for the good, ultimately, of the whole group.

What is needed

Small tasks to perform.

Time required

10 minutes (pair or small-group work) plus 15 minutes (for the pooling of the subgroups' key ideas).

How it works

Students are paired-up or divided into small groups for their five-minute tasks. If they are being asked to focus on a small text – which could either be already in their possession or distributed on the spot – they might be asked to pick out two key themes or words to comment on. If they are being asked to think of 'themes', 'factors' or 'reasons', they could be given small pieces of card on which to scribble down their thoughts; the blank card will emphasize the fact that the students are expected to work hard and fill their card with sensible, intelligent ideas.

A good example in action: International Relations – the oceans

Small groups or pairs are allocated a key question to discuss as follows:

- **Groups 1 and 2**. How do you allocate resources which have previously been considered to be beyond the scope of national appropriation? Refer particularly to the politics of mineral exploration.
- **Groups 3 and 4**. Where does the Law of the Sea end and the Antarctic Treaty begin? Discuss with reference to the regime for the management of the Southern Oceans.
- **Groups 5 and 6**. Discuss the significance of 'creeping jurisdiction' in the Law of the Sea.

Each pair or group focuses on its particular question and then confers with its sister group or pair on links and common themes. Key ideas are jotted down on small pieces of card and then shared with the whole group.

Advantages of this activity

1. There is an excellent – and audible buzz when the students split up into their pairs or groups.
2. Productivity is increased – pairs and small groups can get through a lot of work.
3. Shy, reticent students experience a rise in confidence.
4. The activity generates more ideas, all of which can be pooled for the common good.

Potential problem

Students might start talking about other subjects, so it's a good idea for the tutor to circulate and monitor the conversations!

Main learning outcomes

Students will gain confidence; they will 'own' and 'control' their discussions, and will complete tasks both for their own benefit and that of the other students.

Variation

Pairs can merge into fours, and fours can then join together to form eights – thus sharing and pooling ideas. This procedure is known as 'snowballing' or 'pyramiding' (Habeshaw, Gibbs and Habeshaw, 1992, p.94 and Andresen, 1994, p.28). See also Andresen (1994, p.94) and the 'jigsaw' method (Chalmers and Fuller, 1996, pp. 120–21). For a good summary see Habeshaw, Habeshaw and Gibbs (1992, pp. 45–54) and Gibbs (1992, pp. 9–13).

27

Definitions

In a nutshell

This strategy is particularly useful when the main topic under discussion is highly contentious or hard to define, and thus when a commonly held definition is a vital requirement before meaningful debate can ensue.

Aims

1. To provide all class members with a helpful initial starting point.
2. To emphasize that definitions cannot be taken for granted and can have a considerable effect on discussion.

What is needed

● Felt-tip marker pens.
● A3 paper.
● Blu-tack.

Time required

15 minutes.

How it works

The whole group identifies the key idea or concept that requires attention. The class is then split into two, and each group is given the task of agreeing on a consensus definition. The two definitions are written up on sheets of A3 paper and attached to the wall, and then an overall definition is decided on – a compromise between the two groups' verdicts. At this point, the tutor might want to quote an authoritative source, to offer an accepted academic definition.

A good example in action: Sociology – power

TWO SUBGROUP DEFINITIONS OF 'POWER'

'A type of societal control which can in certain circumstances involve coercion & violence'	'A fundamental aspect of social relationships; in essence, power means power over others'

AUTHORITATIVE DEFINITION

'The chance of a man or a number of men to realise their own will in a communal action even against the resistance of others who are participating in the action.' (Max Weber)

What issues do the student-devised definitions raise? What are their main themes? How do they differ from the 'authoritative' definition?

Advantages of this activity

1. It encourages students to think about 'fundamentals'.
2. It shows that there is no one definition and that there is a large subjective element within academic study.

Potential problem

No consensus may be reached, and controversy might dog the ensuing discussion.

Main learning outcome

Students will be engaged in important debate and will be exposed to a fundamental academic problem – that of defining terms.

28

Essay planning

In a nutshell

This tactic uses the potential of the whole group to discuss and then formally 'plan' an essay answer.

Aims

1. To utilize the insights and ideas of a group to answer a specimen essay question.
2. To discuss the different approaches to essay writing.

What is needed

- A blank board or a blank A3 piece of paper.
- A student scribe.
- Felt-tip marker pens.
- A suitable essay question to tackle.

Time required

20 minutes.

How it works

The tutor introduces an essay question, writes it up for everyone else to see, and then assigns one student to the job of scribe. With contributions from the floor and with a visual focal-point – the board or poster – the tutor can then endeavour to show 'good' and 'bad' ways to approach the same essay question. Approaches to the essay are displayed on the board or poster in note or essay-plan form.

A good example in action: RE – the nature of Islam

Essay question: Discuss the significance of the fusion of state, society and faith in Islam. What is the best way to plan this essay?

- **Approach A:** 'chronological' (an historical survey of how Islam, and the key tenets of Islam, have emerged over the centuries).
- **Approach B**: 'thematic' (an analysis centred around the three specific issues of state, society and faith; their relationship and 'fusion').

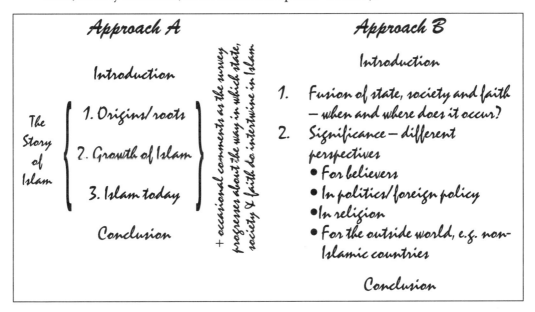

A whole-group discussion could centre around these two main types of approach, with students encouraged to think in terms of approach B and not A.

Advantages of this activity

1. All students are involved in the set task.
2. Good, healthy discussion can take place as ideas about the structure and argument of the essay are floated.
3. It can be stressed throughout that there is no one perfect answer to any one essay; different approaches can be discussed.
4. Students should gain in confidence about answering essay questions as a result of the exercise.

Potential problem

Students tend to have set ways of responding to essay questions; they could therefore become involved in conflict over the best approach, causing those whose ideas are not taken on board to feel alienated.

Main learning outcome

Students will be engaged in the very practical process of essay planning, and their future written assignments should show the benefit of this!

Variation

A large group can be divided into two smaller groups to work on distinct parts or aspects of the essay question. Some related essay planning ideas are explored in Habeshaw, Habeshaw and Gibbs (1992, p.123).

29

The fishbowl*

In a nutshell

This technique alters the arrangement of the group session to create one small discussion group and another group of observers.

Aims

1. To illuminate the nature of group discussion to students.
2. To improve two key academic skills: debate and analysis of debate.

What is needed

- Moveable chairs – to create two circles of students.
- A key issue for discussion.

Time required

15 minutes (discussion) plus 15 minutes (analysis and critique of the discussion) plus 15 minutes (whole-group plenary).

How it works

Two student circles are created – one inside the other – and both circles appoint a

*Source: Habeshaw, Gibbs and Habeshaw, 1992, pp. 90–91 and Gibbs, 1992, pp. 12–13; in one form this technique is known as 'The Fishbowl' (see Gibbs, 1992, pp. 12–13).

chairperson. The inside circle debates a key issue and, after 15 minutes, the second 'outer' circle (whose members have just observed and perhaps made notes about the first discussion) offer their own critique of the debate they have just witnessed. Then the whole class joins together to sum up, evaluate and conclude. The tutor can either join one of the circles as an ordinary member or observe both groups' performance.

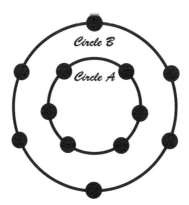

Circle A discusses the set topic for 15 minutes, Circle B offers a critique in the 15 minutes following, and then a whole-group discussion concludes the session.

A good example in action: Psychology – post-war developments

1. Circle A discusses the main areas of post-war developments in psychology – for example, the key landmarks in experimental psychology, perception and human engineering.
2. Circle B then acknowledges these developments, but perhaps shifts the emphasis to other areas – for example, clinical psychology, personality and social psychology.
3. Then the two circles come together to discuss the issue as a whole and to determine in which areas the most important developments took place.

Advantages of this activity

1. Students are encouraged to listen to discussion and produce a critique.
2. The three different discussions can emphasize different points and issues.

Potential problem

Some students might feel ill-at-ease with what they might perceive as the contrived nature of the group set-up.

Main learning outcome

Students will be exposed to three different discussion formats and expected to take on different roles in each.

Variation

Instead of one circle inside another, two circles could exist side by side, and exactly the same process could take place.

30

Editorials

In a nutshell

Ask students to write newspaper editorials on important social, political, economic or historical controversies.

Aims

1. To investigate the issue of bias in key academic debates.
2. To put students into situations where they have to explain and justify certain set arguments.

What is needed

- An 'issue' and a set of varied newspaper titles for which students will have to write their editorials.
- Paper and pens.

Time required

30 minutes (editorial-writing in pairs) plus 20 minutes (reading out of editorials and general group discussion).

How it works

Students are split into pairs; they are given an issue and a newspaper to write for.

They have to discern the bias and style of their publication and the exact opinion which their newspaper would hold on the set issue. They then have to write a real-life editorial (*c.*200 words) and read it out to their classmates. Discussion can then ensue on the issues raised by the various editorials.

A good example in action: History – the Black Death

The students are asked to imagine that the following newspapers were in existence, and publishing, at the time of the Black Death:

- *Daily Telegraph*
- *Sun*
- *Financial Times*
- *European*
- *Guardian*
- *Daily Mail.*

The student pairs are then each allocated a newspaper and asked to write an editorial for it.

Advantages of this activity

1. It makes students think about the key academic issues of bias and perspective.
2. It forces students to confront controversies and 'argue a line'.

Potential problem

Producing a coherent, well written editorial in 30 minutes is a demanding task – help and perhaps even more time could be offered.

Main learning outcome

Students will become aware of key arguments and the importance and influence of tone and bias.

Variation

Students could also be asked to write reports and headlines, or even draw cartoons, to represent specific newspapers' perspectives on key issues.

31

Three planners

In a nutshell

This activity takes the organizational burden off the tutor by asking a trio of students to plan the class session each week.

Aims

1. To involve students not only in classroom activity, but also in the planning of learning sessions.
2. To encourage students to think about what makes a good group session, and to promote format variation.
3. To emphasize to students that it is *their* class – not the tutor's.

What is needed

A rota – to determine which students plan which session.

Time required

The student group should meet together regularly to plan the class in the week preceding the session.

How it works

A rota is organized and each student trio is given a general topic for their group session. They meet for a preliminary chat with the tutor and discuss both the topic and the different activities and methods that are available for formatting the class-room session.

The tutor advises the students on any key texts or issues that must be covered, but the format and schedule of the class are to be decided on by the students. They should be encouraged to vary the approach and to utilize different types of strategy: role-play, groupwork, presentations, visual techniques, worksheets, games and such like. They must advertise their agenda on an OHP and introduce the structure of the session to the other students during the first five minutes of the class.

A good example in action: Geography – the North Wales/South Wales divide

A possible schedule for a student-planned session:

- Introduction to Wales: map at front of class (5 minutes).
- A whole-group discussion focused around the OHP slide: where is the divide? (10 minutes).
- Role-play (the class splits up into two groups; one representing a typical cross-section of North Walians; the other representing South Walians): is the divide real or imaginary? (20 minutes).
- Subgroup work: what are negative implications of the divide? (10 minutes).
- Conclusion (10 minutes).

Advantages of this activity

1. It shifts responsibility on to the students.
2. The students feel that they 'own' the class session and its agenda.
3. Students often have far more interesting and imaginative ideas than staff!
4. Budding teachers might particularly enjoy the challenge and experience involved.

Potential problem

It should be emphasized that the group meeting has to have definite aims and outcomes; students might be slightly neglectful of this, as they might of logistical issues such as timing!

Main learning outcome

Students will gain a sense of responsibility from this exercise and will learn a great deal about structure, planning and communication.

32

Rounds*

In a nutshell

This is a type of activity with several variations and a plethora of uses. At root, it exploits the circular layout of students in a classroom, and at its best can clarify, enable understanding, and also provoke excellent discussion.

Aims

1. To involve all the students – without breaking up the whole group.
2. To make the students, rather than the tutor, the focal point of the class.

What is needed

A circular layout of chairs.

Time required

15 minutes.

How it works

This 15-minute exercise in continual engagement involves students asking the students sitting diametrically opposite questions in sequence (going round the

*Source: Gibbs (1992, pp. 8–9) and Habeshaw, Habeshaw and Gibbs (1992, pp. 65–6).

circle in a clockwise direction). Students have a maximum of one minute to answer their question.

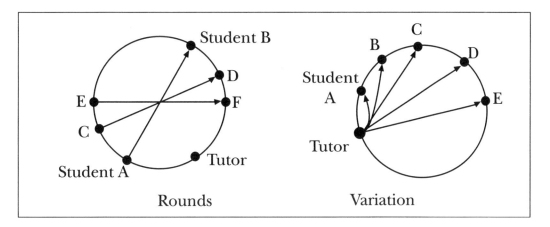

Rounds   Variation

A good example in action: RE – world religions

Questions which students might ask include the following:

- What does the Buddhist term *nirvana* mean?
- Describe what *Kami* are in the Shinto religion?
- To what do Christians refer when they talk about 'the Atonement'?
- Describe the Hindu concept of *karma*.
- Describe how the caste system functions within Hindu society.
- What is meant by the term 'transubstantiation' in Catholicism?
- What is the significance of the Talmud within Judaism?
- Describe the importance of Mecca to Muslims.
- What does the term 'monotheistic' mean and which world religions could be described that way?
- When, and by whom, was the Sikh religion founded?
- What is the importance of the Reformation in Christian history?
- What are the two main forms of Islamic belief and how do they differ?

Advantages of this activity

1. All the students feel actively involved in the exercise.
2. Each student contributes to the understanding of all the other students.
3. The focal point of the exercise is not the tutor – all attention is directed instead on the students involved in the dialogue.

Potential problem

Students might not feel sufficiently confident to engage with each other. Before the exercise it should be stressed that students do have to consider the question for the full 'interchange' minute and not just give up because it is difficult to answer!

Main learning outcomes

Students will be provoked, stimulated and engaged and, by the end of the exercise, they should have gained in understanding and knowledge.

Variation

The tutor chairs a session in which he or she follows through an argument or a theory by going round the circle, engaging each student in turn for a set time (one minute perhaps), asking for contributions or quite definite answers to specific questions. By the time the tutor has gone round the full circle, the group members will have witnessed the exposition of a key theory, an important argument or even a highly relevant chronology.

33

Brainstorming

In a nutshell

This is a much used whole-group strategy and, although it does not demand the creation of subgroups, it can still be highly effective. It should also be pointed out that brainstorming can be enacted in a variety of ways – depending on the nature and the aims of a session.

Aims

1. To involve all students in the pooling of ideas.
2. To enfranchise students, to legitimize their opinions and to increase their oral confidence by accepting all contributions in a non-critical manner.

What is needed

●   A blank board or poster on which to register contributions.
●   A student to act as scribe.

Time required

5 minutes (one of brainstorming's key attributes is its brevity!).

How it works

The tutor identifies the key issue or idea on which the group will concentrate. He or she then asks for immediate responses to this issue or idea – whether intellectual or emotional, well thought-out or highly spontaneous. All contributions are written up by the student scribe, so that the collection of responses and impressions remains visible, and acts as a reminder, or spur, for the class.

A good example in action: English – themes in Nick Hornby's *High Fidelity* (1995)

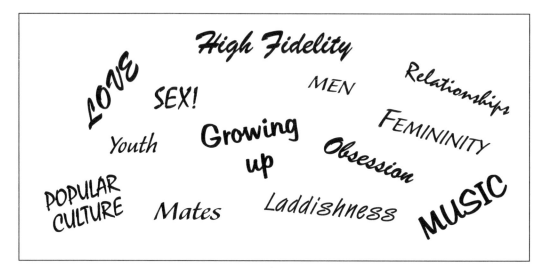

Advantages of this activity

1. All students can feel confident about getting involved, as their ideas will not be scrutinized immediately for cogency or quality.
2. There are no right or correct responses.
3. There is an important and healthy visual element: for the rest of the session, students and the tutor not only can refer to the brainstormed responses, but can also use them to provoke and stimulate discussion.

Potential problem

Spontaneous discussion – and dissension – might sabotage the short-and-sweet brainstorming exercise.

Main learning outcome

Students will have been exposed to a huge variety of responses and reflections, and discussion and debate will have been catalysed around these ideas.

Variation

Brainstormed contributions do not have to be written up for the whole group to see. Indeed, in the circumstances of very contentious points being raised, it might be positively advantageous not to give legitimacy to controversial ideas by writing them up.

34

Press releases

In a nutshell

This is a strategy inspired by the 'spin-doctor' world of 1990s politics, with students assigned the task of writing well focused and highly important press releases.

Aims

1. To involve students in thinking about issues from different angles.
2. To encourage students to think about how actions and beliefs are justified and explained in the modern media-dominated world.

What is needed

Paper and pens.

Time required

20 minutes (writing of press releases) plus 20 minutes (discussion).

How it works

The tutor introduces the key issue or event being considered. Students are then split up into pairs and asked to produce and write a press release on behalf of an important person, movement or organization involved in the set topic.

The press release must justify and rationalize the possibly controversial actions or behaviour of the person, movement or organization. The student pairs might be given different people or groups to write for, or they might be given the same. The groups then read out their press releases in turn to the whole group.

A good example in action: Law – US law and the O.J. Simpson case

Event: O.J. Simpson has just been acquitted and student subgroups are asked to write press releases on behalf of the following different clients:

- Group A: the defence team
- Group B: the prosecution team
- Group C: the judge
- Group D: the jury.

What key arguments will each press release seek to emphasize? What will be the tone of each? What will be the aims of each statement? Who will the press release be aimed at?

The groups are then asked to respond to each other's press releases. What do these press releases reveal about the case and the legal issues involved?

Advantages of this activity

1. It combines role-play with groupwork and involves a sizeable written element.
2. It can illuminate the main perspectives on key issues.
3. It highlights the key political skills of propaganda and publicity.

Potential problems

The time limit may be quite a challenge, and students may find it difficult to write their statements in the appropriate language and style.

Main learning outcomes

Students will be engaged in a highly creative and stimulating exercise and will analyse a key issue from a specific perspective.

Variation

Instead of press releases why not try party political broadcasts! Small student groups could spend time together preparing a broadcast. Then, the number of students required can 'act out' and 'deliver' this statement for the whole group to see.

Summary and evaluation

This chapter has clearly shown that, for tutors in the humanities and social sciences, there are many groupwork variations and possibilities. Tutors can use both whole-group and small-group situations to promote discussion and, if activities and exercises are well planned, groupwork can be particularly effective in involving and enthusing students.

In an era of increasing class sizes, groupwork tactics can be particularly economical and productive. Whether the choice is simple buzz groups or one of the other, more intricate, small-group arrangements, students can benefit enormously from group-centred techniques. For subjects such as History, English, Sociology and Politics which are overtly discussion-based, small-group work, and controlled whole-group strategies can bring significant dividends.

With small-group strategies there are many advantages. First, students can talk with other students and do not have the 'intimidating' presence of the tutor to reckon with. Second, the evidence of students' own opinions suggests that group-work has a very special merit: it enables students to meet other students and to come out of isolation. Tutors may be undecided about whether small groups should have a constant 'trusting' membership or whether membership should be more 'random', but, either way, small groups can become good, intimate and very sociable arenas for discussion.

For staff too there is the wonderful feeling of splitting students up into smaller groups and immediately hearing a very healthy 'buzz'! This is a priceless commodity! Even if some small-group discussions do turn to football and the previous night's TV, and even if small groups become dominated by outspoken students just as some large groups can, the noise of small-group activity is far more appealing than horrible whole-group silences.

From the comments of staff it is clear that some fear abandoning students, or at least being seen to have abandoned students. For many tutors the idea of a back-seat role is perhaps unnatural – but surely the art of enabling discussion is as much of a skill as offering unadulterated expertise? Students can certainly be liberated and enfranchised by groupwork tactics.

5　Role-play

With role-play everyone can become involved. When students enjoy role-play they want to study more about the topic.
Professor Keith Laybourn, Professor of History, University of Huddersfield

Introduction

Role-play is a well known and frequently used groupwork strategy. In fundamental terms role-play means drama, with students asked to take on and act out set roles – perhaps politicians in a Cabinet meeting or ordinary people in an everyday scene. Students are expected to learn by empathizing with a role and from having to understand and explain a specific 'position'.

There are, however, a plethora of role-play variants, and it is these options and alternatives that this chapter seeks to introduce and explore.

I would like to thank Philip Woodfine, Keith Laybourn, Brendan Evans, Derek Lynch, Judith Ashurst, Rhys Davies, Bill Stafford, Peter Greenleaf, Adrian Hickerton and Lisa Cox for their assistance with this chapter.

Related activities

The following activities, outlined and explained in other chapters, also include an important 'role-play' element:

35

The press conference

In a nutshell

Here we have a simple, but dramatic, 'event'. One person – a key writer or states-person perhaps – is put on the spot to answer hard-hitting questions, with all the accompanying controversy, theatre and drama. It is a real event – a real confrontation.

Aims

1. To bring out the important issues, the key arguments and the academic debates surrounding the central personality.
2. To provoke the question-askers into devising questions from specific and well defined perspectives.

What is needed

● One student, to play the central figure.
● The other students to play journalists.
● A 'date' to add to the 'authenticity' of the press conference (for example, the day after a famous event, a controversial incident or the publication of a famous book or piece of writing).

Time required

20 minutes (press conference) plus 10 minutes (plenary discussion).

105

How it works

One student is asked (either at the beginning of the class or at the end of the preceding session) to play the role of a key personality. This figure will usually be central to the main topic under discussion and the accompanying lectures; it may be a politician, a character in a play or novel, a philosopher or perhaps just a significant person in the epoch or context under consideration.

The other students are also asked to take part. Three will act as specific journalists – maybe from different British newspapers or from different countries (in both these cases the journalists will have quite distinct angles on the story). They will bombard the famous or controversial figure with relevant and varied questions (prepared either spontaneously, in small groups at the beginning of the class, or during the week prior to the session). The tutor should act as chair and ask questions as appropriate; the other students should also think up pertinent questions to throw in. A ten-minute plenary discussion should round off the exercise, with students coming out of their set roles.

A good example in action: Economics – *The Wealth of Nations*

The year is 1776. Adam Smith publishes *An Inquiry Into The Nature and Causes Of The Wealth Of Nations*. He is greeted by three specially chosen journalists, who represent *The Economist, The Scotsman* and *The Times*. Whereas the journalist from *The Economist* is interested primarily in the economic theories advanced in the book, *The Scotsman* is fascinated by the local angle to the story and *The Times* is eager to explore the broader implications of the book's publication.

The layout for the 'press conference' is as follows:

Adam Smith ☐

☐ Tutor

☐ ☐ ☐ ☐ ☐
☐ ☐ ☐ ☐ ☐
Journalists

Advantages of this activity

1. Students are put on the spot and asked to think and act in set roles.
2. The press conference contains an important element of drama and theatre!
3. The three journalists have to produce specific questions relevant to their key newspaper or national interests.

Potential problem

Stage fright is a possibility – the four key actors must be well chosen! The other students – the audience – must also be encouraged to ask questions.

Main learning outcome

Students will have to consider their questions carefully in terms of obtaining answers that cast light on the real issues at play.

Variations

1. **Dimbleby.** One journalist (the 'Dimbleby' figure) grills the central personality for 10 minutes (both roles are played by students). The audience then joins in – with each student in the audience given a particular role to play and asked to ask questions from a particular perspective. Thus, questions should rain in from all angles! The Dimbleby figure at the front chairs the event.
2. **'Hot-seating'.** *This is English without the drama. The student takes on the role of a character in the text and they are grilled. They are in the hot seat! But they're told in advance, in order that adequate preparation can take place.*
    Maggie Sheen, Deputy Head and English teacher, Pudsey Grangefield High School
3. **Question Time.** *I had a Question Time on British politics in 1832 – four key personalities from the era were involved. There was a host and the whole programme was videoed. It was an excellent occasion – and the pupils got a lot out of it.*
    Rhys Davies, History Teacher, Tytherington High School, Macclesfield

36

The set debate

In a nutshell

A controversial academic issue is debated by two sets of opposing and well prepared student protagonists. What emerges is a very healthy slanging match!

Aims

1. To bring alive a crucial two-sided argument.
2. To give students a line to argue and to make them argue this – even if they do not agree with it!

What is needed

- Two sets of protagonists.
- Moveable chairs.
- A chairman (the tutor or a particularly authoritative student).

Time required

30 minutes (debate) plus 10 minutes (plenary discussion).

How it works

The classroom is split in two: one group of students to the left, another to the right. The chair introduces the debate and asks the spokespeople for the two principal views to introduce their perspective on the question. A cut-and-thrust discussion can then take place for a good half-hour before the two spokespeople sum up their positions and the chair concludes the session. After the debate the participants can come out of their set debating roles; they can then reveal their own individual thoughts and discuss how the debate changed, or did not change, their own personal views.

A good example in action: Psychology – psychodynamic theory and object relations theory

This debate centres around which theory best explains the human personality. The two perspectives are as follows:

- **Argument A:** Freud's psychodynamic theory which states that the personality consists of three main parts (id, ego and superego) is sound.
- **Argument B:** Freud's theory is flawed and unconvincing; Klein's notion of object relations is more plausible and persuasive.

The student group is divided in two, one half putting forward Argument A and the other half Argument B. A plenary session can follow, with students 'out of role' discussing the merits of the two arguments.

Advantages of this activity

1. It can simplify and clarify a vital academic debate.
2. It forces a helpful contrast between distinct views.
3. Students have to argue views that they may not agree with personally.

Potential problems

Students may be tempted to give up on their view and say, 'I'm only arguing this because the tutor told me to!' Here, the tutor must emphasize that it is a crucial skill to be able to argue a 'line' that one does not personally agree with! Certain students may also dominate on each side of the debate – the chair must be encouraged to bring in the quieter students.

Main learning outcome

Students will be involved and engaged in an important debate, and will have been exposed to both sides of an argument.

Variation

'Polarization' or 'confrontation' games are another version of this activity. These work best with large classes – perhaps 20, rather than ten students. The tutor stands in the middle of the room and acts as questionmaster, having prepared a set of extremely contentious statements – for example, on a Third World politics course, 'The IMF is a consistent hindrance to Third World development'.

The only two options are 'I agree' or 'I disagree', but students have very little, or no, time to think! They have to go immediately to either side of the classroom in accordance with their answer: for example, all the 'yes' people go to the left; all the 'no' people go to the right. Two minutes of full-throttle debate follow, during which time students are allowed to change their mind, or can have their mind changed! Anyone who does alter their opinion on the issue has, symbolically, to cross the room into the opposing lobby.

During the debate, some people will get on their soapbox and try to convert the others. In a normal class there will always be those students who are sure of their opinions and others who are not so sure. People are allowed to change their mind!

This is an entertaining and funny device. The rule is that you can't speak more than twice in the debate, and such confrontation games are particularly good with highly controversial or emotive issues. For instance, I was involved in a really excellent one about the ethics of abortion.
Martin Davies, former SCM Northern Regional Secretary, Manchester

37

Role-play – international diplomacy

In a nutshell

This activity brings a key event or era alive via role-play.

Aims

1. To involve all students in acting out a vital scenario and contributing to the class.
2. To highlight the important nuances – often spatial – inherent in diplomacy.

What is needed

- A landmark issue.
- Country 'labels' (prepared by the tutor in advance).
- Movable furniture.
- Students to 'play' countries.

Time required

30 minutes (role-play) plus 20 minutes (plenary discussion).

How it works

The tables in the classroom are moved to create an imaginary map of Europe, or the world, or whichever other area is under the spotlight. Each table represents a country, and the students, perhaps in groups of two or three, are allocated a specific country to play. They sit at their country's table. To kick off, one table is asked to introduce their country and their country's general diplomatic outlook at a key landmark moment – for example, on the verge of a key alliance or in the aftermath of an important historical event. Thereafter, all the other countries are asked to explain their diplomatic attitudes. Role-plays such as this can either be spontaneous (set up at the beginning of a class with students who were expecting a normal session) or organized (with students preparing their role over a three or four-week cycle).

A good example in action: History – Bismarck's alliance system 1871–90

Students rearrange the classroom tables so as to create an 'imaginary' map of Europe (see figure below). Two or three students sit at each table and take on the role of spokespeople for their allotted country. The furniture rearrangement has the effect of altering the atmosphere and improving the classroom dynamics. The mock map creates a real, positive spatial effect. The main elements of Bismarck's controversial diplomacy can then be explored.

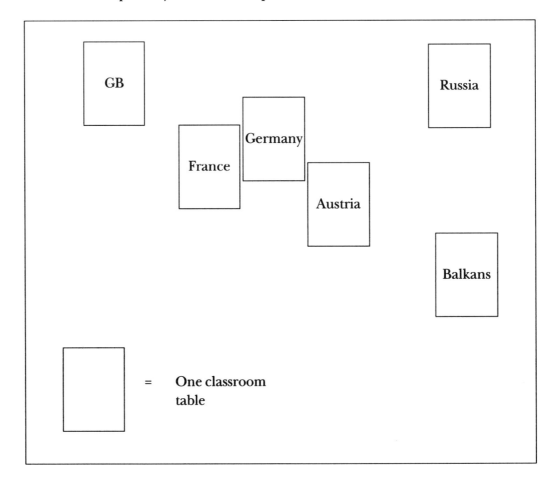

Advantages of this activity

1. The furniture rearrangement alters the atmosphere and dynamics.
2. The new room layout can foster an improved awareness of the key diplomatic issues and themes.
3. It's good fun!

Potential problems

Moving furniture might be logistically difficult – but all efforts should be made! Also, because taking a chronological journey through a key period might be slightly one-dimensional, a more thematic plenary at the end of the session might be in order.

Main learning outcome

The spatial dimension to this set-up is exciting, provocative and full of possibilities, and students will gain important insights into the group dynamics of diplomacy or other types of history.

Variations

This type of role-play obviously has endless variants. It can be used to illuminate important events (such as the Russian Revolution – complete with Bolsheviks, Mensheviks, Tsarists, Provisional Government politicians and foreign statesmen), storylines or plots in a work of fiction (such as a novel or play), or eras (such as the French Revolution and its different players – King, Queen and Court, Girondins, Jacobins, the foreign powers and the *émigrés*).

When students are in role-play character, why not ask them to write letters ... to themselves firstly, and then to other people involved in the role-play? This can be a very stimulating exercise.

Martin Davies, former SCM Northern Regional Secretary, Manchester

38

Set oral roles

In a nutshell

Change the atmosphere, and 'ownership', of a group session by allocating all the key roles to students ... including chair, presenter and discussant.

Aims

1. To liberate students by cutting down on tutor input and involvement.
2. To give students ownership, and to transfer the onus of making the session work on to them.

What is needed

● A set topic.
● A rota for the roles: chair, presenter and discussant.

Time required

One hour.

How it works

At the beginning of term all the students in a group are put on a rota and during the term each is designated a set of roles – chair, presenter, discussant and participant (each student takes all four roles at least once during the term). At each class, the chair introduces the topic, the presenter presents a paper and the discussant – who has had a copy of the paper prior to the class – puts forward a critique or response. It is then the chair's duty to keep the class going, and to perhaps vary its format if the situation demands it. The tutor joins the student circle and does nothing other than contribute minimally when appropriate. The chair then summarizes the session at the end.

Ideally, whole-group sessions should be hosted by the students involved – and the chair is fully entitled to change and alter the format of the class during the hour.

A good example in action: Geography – explore the main aspects of social planning

SCHEDULE

● The chairperson introduces the main issues – the consequences of physical planning, the identification of problem areas, and the need for facilities to respond to defined needs (5 minutes).
● The presenter presents a paper (10 minutes).
● The discussant responds to the paper (10 minutes).
● A group debate is led by the chairperson. This involves all the participants and aims to investigate and evaluate the main contours of social planning (25 minutes).

Advantages of this activity

1. Students 'own' the class and its agenda.
2. Everyone has to prepare thoroughly – or they could be embarrassed!
3. Transferable skills are emphasized.

Potential problem

An inadequate or unprepared student chair can undermine a session and can necessitate greater tutor involvement than desired.

Main learning outcome

Students will learn that the session is 'theirs', and that it is their responsibility to make it work.

39

Shock tactics

In a nutshell

This activity is designed to shake up a group session that has proven to be particularly low key and predictable. It is, in essence, a tactic of staff role-play, with the tutor's performance provoking the students into action.

Aims

1. To provoke and stimulate students by means of a pre-planned staff role-play.
2. To make students aware of one particularly important viewpoint, and to make this view accessible and familiar.

What is needed

A plan of action for the tutor!

Time required

10 minutes at the start of a class.

How it works

The tutor walks into the classroom, speech in hand, orating from the moment he or she enters in a heavily dramatic fashion. He or she continues to talk, ignoring all the usual formalities associated with the beginning of a class. The students will be shocked and surprised, particularly when they listen to the tutor's words. The tutor's speech may include such a phrase as 'and I resign herewith', and, although this phrase may come from within a famous play, novel or historical or political speech, the words might carry a shocking real-life resonance to the students. When the tutor eventually 'comes clean' the atmosphere of the class will have been affected for the better. The class can then continue, with the students already engaged by the dramatic, theatrical entry...

A good example in action: Politics – Thatcherism

SPEECH BY SIR GEOFFREY HOWE – LONDON, 13 NOVEMBER 1990

It has been suggested – even, indeed, by some of my friends – that I decided to resign solely because of questions of style and not on matters of substance at all . . . The conflict of loyalty . . . has become all too great. I no longer believe it possible to resolve that conflict. . . . That is why I have resigned. . . . The time has come for others to consider their own response to the tragic conflict of loyalties with which I have myself wrestled for perhaps too long.
MacArthur, 1993, pp. 471–5

Advantages of this activity

1. It's different!
2. An extreme view or position is brought to life, is made accessible – and has to be confronted.

Potential problem

The tutor may lack the ability to pull it off!

Main learning outcome

Students will have been immediately provoked and engaged in an important debate.

Variation

A tutor could take on a particularly extreme, controversial or provocative position throughout a full-class session. A tutor consistently pushing a Marxist line, for example, could help to create a healthy dynamic in the class. Debate should hopefully flourish!

40

'Question Time'

In a nutshell

Tie up a course, a module or term with an end-of-semester 'Question Time' event featuring all the key personalities from the course – to reflect on the big topics and the dominant themes, and to crystallize debate on the really fundamental issues.

Aims

1. To enable students to see, grapple with, and grasp the key underlying themes and continuities within a course.
2. To engender make-believe and hypothetical situations in which personalities who wouldn't normally have met each other do so, with all the accompanying interest.

What is needed

Six students with sufficient knowledge and confidence to role-play the chosen personalities.

Time required

30 minutes

How it works

Pick out the six most dominating, influential and interesting personalities from all periods or phases of a course. Ask six students to play these personalities. They could each be given a week to read about, and familiarize themselves with, their famous individual. At the session a whole-group discussion could take place initially, with students asked to think about the different attitudes and perspectives personified by the six figures. The six role-players are then invited to position themselves at the front (*à la Question Time*) and are asked in turn to introduce themselves. The session is then thrown open to the other members of the class (themselves situated in the 'audience', and ready with questions). The added spice is the fact that personalities who, in reality, would never have met now have the chance to question *each other*. After the last audience question, each member of the panel is given the chance to sum up.

Finally, a debriefing session is held at which the six students – out of character – and those in the audience are asked to reflect on the main themes that ran through the event.

A good example in action: Media Studies – the media in the 1990s

Invited guests:
1.   Ted Turner
2.   Lord Beaverbrook
3.   Rupert Murdoch
4.   Richard Branson
5.   Lord Rothermere
6.   Kelvin McKenzie.

Six 'celebrities'

tutor ☐   ☐ ☐ ☐ ☐ ☐ ☐

☐ ☐ ☐ ☐ ☐ ☐

Question-askers

What would these six people be asked about? The history, and future, of broadcasting? Pay-per-view TV? The issues involved in newspaper ownership? How different would their views be?

Advantages of this activity

1.   There is a refreshing hypothetical element.
2.   It crystallizes key issues and themes.
3.   People will be relaxed – and profound points will emerge.

Potential problem

Because of the set-up students may fail to take the event seriously.

Main learning outcome

Students will be able to analyse the relationships between people they may never have seen together before; the actors will be exposed to serious questioning and they will have had to think on their feet and respond intelligently.

41

Sculpting

In a nutshell

Get a group of students to act out and 'freeze' a famous scene from history, from a novel, or from contemporary politics. Then ask other students to throw questions at the people involved in the sculpture.

Aims

1. To re-enact, and thus access, a key event or scene, and to enable those involved to acquire empathy with the situation.
2. To involve all students – either in the sculpture or in asking questions of the actors.

What is needed

A blown-up photo or picture to guide both those involved in the sculpture and those watching its creation.

Time required

15 minutes ('sculpting' and questions) plus 10 minutes (discussion).

How it works

The tutor brings a particularly significant picture, photograph or image to the class with the intention of re-enacting it. If, say, the set picture incorporates five people, five students are asked to act out and 'freeze' these characters' positions, as in the picture. When this has taken place, the other students ask questions of those involved in the sculpture, such as: 'How do you feel?', 'What are your motivations here?', 'What's going to happen next?' The 'freeze' is then halted and a plenary discussion ensues, with the actors coming out of character and entering into an evaluation of the process and the issues raised.

A good example in action: RE – The Last Supper

POSSIBLE QUESTIONS

To Jesus:
- 'What is the meaning of this event?'
- 'How are you feeling?'
- 'What's going to happen in the future?'

To the disciples:
- 'Why are you here?'
- 'What is the significance of this gathering?'
- 'What are your feelings towards Jesus at this moment?'

(N.B. In a class of 12 people, it will obviously not be possible to have a full set of disciples; perhaps there could be five, plus Jesus, and thus six question-askers.)

Advantages of this activity

1. Students have to move around, and the atmosphere in the classroom will change as a result – always a beneficial development!
2. The scene is brought to life, and the student onlookers learn about, and question, the main characters in the sculpture.

Potential problem

Some students may experience all the usual embarrassment about doing drama.

Main learning outcome

Students will empathize with, and will act themselves into, key roles, thereby gaining an understanding of the main issues involved 'from the inside'.

42

Simulation – mock meetings

In a nutshell

This is a formal reconstruction of a key event or meeting, with all students taking the part of players in the drama.

Aims

1. To reconstruct and bring to life an important event.
2. To make students understand the process and procedures involved in formal events.

What is needed

●   Relevant newspaper cuttings and other sources – to be studied before the class, so that all the participants can gain helpful and necessary insights into the workings of the meeting.
●   Name-tags or badges to denote the characters.

Time required

30 minutes (simulation) plus 20 minutes (plenary discussion).

How it works

The details of the key event are studied before the class, and all students are asked to research one assigned role. They come to the class prepared and, with the tutor in attendance, the meeting is acted out, to an ultimate conclusion.

A good example in action: Media Studies – the Press Complaints Commission

The PCC meets to discuss the behaviour of the British Press in the aftermath of Princess Diana's death. Students are challenged to simulate the proceedings of the PCC on the basis of newspaper reports and other briefing documents (studied prior to the class).

The following roles are played by students:

- Chairman
- Deputy Chairman
- current editor of a broadsheet newspaper
- journalist on a foreign newspaper
- ex-editor of a tabloid newspaper
- former MP
- a university professor of journalism
- the former press officer to the Prime Minister
- a reporter on an upmarket tabloid
- a member of the public (male)
- another member of the public (female)
- secretary.

(The tutor gives specific 'real' names to these characters in advance of the simulation, so the students know exactly who they are playing.)

The chairman introduces the controversy involving the press reportage of Princess Diana's death and then chairs the ensuing debate.

At the end of the simulation, the group must work together to issue a statement on behalf of the PCC which outlines its general position and its specific recommendations.

Advantages of this activity

1. Complex scenarios are brought to life, clarified and illuminated.
2. All students have a role and feel involved.

Potential problem

The absence of any student from class on the appointed day can sabotage the whole event.

Main learning outcomes

Students will acquire an extremely useful understanding of how important historical and political events proceed and, in particular, the nature of decision-making processes; they will also become aware of the relationships and interrelationships between the characters in the simulation.

Variation

Any type of event or meeting could be reconstructed in this way – a Cabinet meeting, a business forum or even an episode in a novel.

43

The courtroom

In a nutshell

Create a courtroom situation and designate students to play the key roles. Use the court to adjudicate upon a key academic debate, issue or controversy. What is the verdict? What do the students make of the verdict?

Aims

1.   To bring a key debate or controversy to life.
2.   To identify the main arguments at play within an issue.

What is needed

● A controversy to put under the spotlight.
● An open-plan room, to reorganize as a courtroom.

Time required

30 minutes (courtroom case) plus 20 minutes (plenary discussion).

How it works

The students are allocated set courtroom roles: judge, jury members, witnesses, the prosecution and the defence. Before the role-play the tutor and the students discuss all the roles to be played. The 'judge' in particular has a very important part: he or she needs to be in control and should bring in the various actors as and when appropriate.

At the end of the role-play the jury gives its 'verdict', and the judge sums up. Then a plenary discussion – with the students out of role – can bring out the key issues and themes to emerge from the drama.

A good example in action: English – *Of Mice and Men*

Characters to be played by students:

- George – the defendant
- spokesperson for the prosecution
- spokesperson for the defence
- the judge
- witnesses: Lennie, Slim, Curley, Crooks, Candy
- jury members (three).

The judge chairs the proceedings and asks the participants to contribute when appropriate; at the end of the process the jury members are asked to reach a verdict.

Advantages of this activity

1. It simplifies and dramatizes a key academic debate.
2. It involves all the students.
3. The 'jury' comes to a verdict based on evidence – just as students have to come to a judgement based on evidence when writing their essays.

Potential problem

The tutor and the students need to be sure how the courtroom will operate and how the 'trial' will proceed.

Main learning outcome

Students will take an active part in an important academic debate, and this involvement should improve their understanding.

Summary and evaluation

Role-play is perhaps the most obvious non-conventional groupwork strategy. It is a technique that many students will have experienced at school, and may also go on to experience in the world of work. Although some staff, and some students, are sceptical about the value of acting out very unnatural roles, the empathy value implicit in role-play, and the general energy it can give to a class, should not be underestimated.

In subjects like History, English and Politics – with a high 'people' content – role-play can certainly be a very appropriate strategy, illuminating the nature and character of vital personalities, events and eras. And, as this chapter has shown, role-play has many guises: 'sculptures' and 'set debates' – to name but two variants – add to the massive richness and potential of this technique.

However, role-play as a small-group activity also raises many questions. Should it be organized, planned and finely tuned over a definite time period or should it be thrust on to a class spontaneously? Is role-play merely an extension of a childish game or can quite profound insights emerge from sessions? Is it appropriate for all topics or does it have its limitations?

The truth is that role-play has its passionate enthusiasts and its damning detractors. On the plus side it can be viewed as overtly interactive, highly enjoyable and plain good fun! Role-play gives everyone a part and therefore engages even the quietest of students. It is also true that fundamentally important points can be brilliantly illuminated by role-play sessions.

Critics, however, argue that role-play can too easily descend into a shallow farce, and that the main issues at stake can get lost. In addition, many topics do not, by their intrinsic nature, lend themselves to role-play. Some people – both staff and students – are embarrassed by role-play, and others are frightened. In this view, role-play is both too contrived and too daunting.

The overall conclusion must be that role-play can be the best, and the worst, strategy. It can bring excellent involvement, passionate participation and profound outcomes. But it can also alienate and worry people. Ultimately, however, any tactic which can bring alive characters, issues and events must have its place in a tutor's 'tool kit'.

Part II

Activities for difficult territory

In one sense, codifying activities by genre is akin to 'putting the cart before the horse', since, often, the tutor's thinking before a class is not 'I fancy a role-play today – what kind should I use?', but rather, 'I've got a difficult topic today – how can I be imaginative, bring it alive and make it more interesting than usual?'

In this Part, therefore, the focus shifts to what I have labelled 'difficult territory' or, more accurately, three particularly difficult types of territory – namely, abstract ideas, primary documents and numerical data. Groupwork sessions in the humanities and social sciences often have to delve into these difficult areas. The key questions are these: how can 'difficult territory' be traversed? What practical strategies can be employed?

The message of the following chapters and activities is that it *is* possible to be imaginative and creative in the fields of abstract ideas, primary documents and numerical data, and it *is* possible to produce better-than-normal discussion through set-piece activities.

6   Abstract ideas

If you try you can make everything interesting. Ideas, for example, are dry and difficult, but it can be done. You've got to look for small steps.
Christine Bell, Staff Development Officer, Learning Consultancy Group, University of Huddersfield

Introduction

Many topics in humanities and social science subjects revolve around abstract ideas and theoretical concepts. Whether it is political theorists trying to explain Marxism, philosophers discussing feminism, historians grappling with Nazism or economists analysing monetarism, the aim is the same: to clarify, to understand and to discuss.

In the course of writing this book, I have been told by several people that concepts and theories do not lend themselves to imaginative classroom methods and, similarly, that it is almost impossible to make ideas interesting. The view seems to be that abstract ideas can only be understood through high-powered, intellectual discussion. Because of this, abstract ideas can often remain closed and inaccessible to students. They seem to be cloaked in some kind of mystique. Somehow, the view is that it is not possible to simplify abstract ideas, effectively implying that some academic topics are 'above' others and that some, by their very nature, can defy imaginative tutors. I hope that this chapter goes some way to challenging this rather pessimistic consensus.

I would like to thank John Fazey, Mike Murcott, Judith Ashurst, Derek Lynch and Linda Franklin for their assistance with this chapter.

Related activities

44

Role-playing ideas

In a nutshell

Dispense with the normal 'discussion' of ideas and, instead, bring ideas alive via role-play. Create a realistic everyday situation and insert protagonists (role-play characters) whose task it is to personify and illuminate distinct ideas – ideas which have already been outlined and highlighted in other class sessions. Act out a 'situation' and see the different ideological positions emerge.

Aims

1. To illuminate, and make accessible, key ideas and ideological perspectives.
2. To show the interplay and potential conflict between ideas.
3. To involve students in a real-life, familiar situation, and to create empathy between 'actor' and 'role'.

What is needed

- A real-life situation (to be devised by the tutor).
- Students to play the set roles.
- Other students to watch the scenario develop and analyse the interaction of different ideas.

Time required

15 minutes (role-play) plus 15 minutes (reflection on the role-play).

How it works

The tutor introduces the general topic and identifies the key ideas under the spotlight. Students are asked, or volunteer, to play the key characters in the role-play. The class discusses the key ideas under consideration, and the tutor familiarizes the 'actors' with the 'scene' in which they have to make the ideas come alive. The actors put their full efforts into illuminating the ideas in words and actions. The 'non-actors' observe as the role-play takes place. The tutor closes the scene, and the class comes together to reflect on the role-play and the abstract ideas which emerged.

A good example in action: Politics – industrial relations

A chocolate factory is in dispute: the owner (a typically entrepeneurial and free-market capitalist) is confronted by the shop steward (a person who, outside working hours, is an activist in the local Labour Party). As the role-play begins, only the owner knows the details of the controversy: ten staff are to be made compulsorily redundant as a necessary cost-cutting exercise. He has to tell the shop steward and the workforce of his decision. The conversation begins...

Questions that need to be considered after the role-play:

- What is the capitalist's philosophy?
- What is the capitalist's reaction?
- How does the socialist respond?
- What is the nature of trade unionism?
- Is there such a thing as working-class solidarity?

Advantages of this activity

1. Ideas are brought to life in a 'concrete', 'non-abstract', 'everyday' context.
2. Students are involved in three different areas – acting, observing and discussing.

Potential problem

The role-players must have the confidence to improvise.

Main learning outcome

Students will witness a real-life encounter between different ideas and ideological positions; ideas will be made more accessible.

Variation

On the subject of abstract ideas we do a case called What is democracy? We telephone(!) six dead philosophers and ask them for their different views on what democracy is. Do you need representation? Do you need participation? Again the class can work via presentation or small-group work. You could also role-play the philosophers. You just need a way into the topic. But the students have also got to read around the subject. There are, fundamentally, no short-cuts. It's not just fun – but you do need a way-in – in order to provoke the right kind of discussion.
Dr Martin Cloonan, Case Studies, Department of Politics, University of York

45

Draw an idea!

In a nutshell

Complement the intellectualizing and verbalizing that usually accompanies the discussion of abstract ideas by asking students to represent 'ideas' in a pictorial or diagrammatic form. Use the diagrams and images produced by students as a stimulus to further discussion.

Aims

1. To make abstract ideas more accessible and less intimidating, thus helping students to manipulate and understand ideas better.
2. To tap into many students' well developed graphic skills, and to emphasize that learning can take place via pictorial representation.

What is needed

- Felt-tip marker pens.
- A3 paper.
- Blu-tack.

Time required

10 minutes (drawing) plus 15 minutes (discussion based on the pictorial representations).

How it works

Students are asked individually (or in pairs) to represent an abstract idea in pictorial, graphic or diagrammatic form. Refreshingly, this exercise is subsumed in subjectivity – it is clear that there is no single or correct way to visualize or depict an abstract concept. After ten minutes all the pictorial representations are displayed on the wall, and further discussion can follow. Several questions could then be raised:

- Is there a common thread evident in all the representations?
- What are the general themes?
- What problems are inherent in this exercise?

A good example in action: Economics – oligopoly

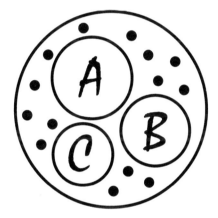

This is one student's representation of oligopoly. How could this image stimulate debate? How would someone else depict the same concept?

In the image, the student is clearly trying to show the essence of oligopoly – a small group of dominant producers ('A', 'B' and 'C') in a market (the big circle), with also a series of minor producers at large (the dots) – totally dwarfed by the three dominant firms.

Other students may represent oligopoly in a different manner. Nonetheless, the question is: what issues does this particular image raise? Furthermore, is it accurate to view oligopoly as three dominant firms and numerous small ones? Is there any way in which the representation could be improved? What general issues are raised by the topic of oligopoly?

Advantages of this activity

1. It varies the usual currency of debate – from words to images.
2. It enables students to express themselves in a new, perhaps more natural, manner.

3. Drawing images deformalizes the atmosphere – encouraging students to open up and fostering quite spontaneous discussion.

Potential problems

It must be emphasized there is no right or wrong way to depict ideas, but this subjec tivity could, in itself, cause problems – for example, how can an idea be pinned down? In addition, some students might not take the exercise seriously. To avoid this, the aim and legitimacy of the exercise must be explained beforehand.

Main learning outcomes

Students will realize that ideas can be explained in a non-verbal form and will gain confidence in assessing and comprehending ideas.

46

Manifesto writing

In a nutshell

You are studying a key historical or political development, in which various movements – whether political, religious or economic – are involved. This activity is about exploring the subject further by asking students to produce 'manifestos' or 'responses' from different and distinct perspectives.

Aims

1. To illuminate the many different perspectives on important issues.
2. To encourage students to penetrate distinct mindsets and understand ideas and ideological positions.

What is needed

- Felt-tip marker pens.
- A3 paper.
- Blu-tack.

Time required

20 minutes (small-group manifesto writing) plus 15 minutes (whole-group discussion about the manifestos).

How it works

A key issue is identified, on which there are obvious and distinct perspectives. Small groups of students are asked to produce a manifesto on the set issue from a given perspective. The manifestos are written up on posters and displayed on the classroom walls. A whole-group discussion follows.

A good example in action: History of Ideas – socialism

Students are divided into the following groups:

- New Labour 'Blairites' (*c.*1997)
- Utopian Socialists (early nineteenth century)
- Bolshevik Party (*c.*1917)
- German Social Democrats (late nineteenth century)
- Attlee's post-war Labour government (1945).

Each group has to produce a 'manifesto' to outline the contours of their specific brand of socialism.

A typical student-produced manifesto is illustrated below.

Bolshevik Party (c. 1917)

We believe in socialism, pure socialism, with no compromises & no limitations. We believe that key industries should be put under state control & that a vanguard of our strategists should govern on behalf of the workers. Our five key principles are these:

1. Equality
2. Fraternity
3. Solidarity
4. State control of the means of production
5. World Revolution

What issues are raised by the manifestos? What do they have in common? Where do they differ? Are there any fundamental core traits of socialism?

Potential problem

Students might not know enough about the 'perspective' that they have been allocated, and thus preliminary discussion, and the tutor's help, may be needed.

Main learning outcomes

Students will have gained an appreciation of set positions and the ability to prioritize key ideas.

47

A Post-it wall

In a nutshell

Get to grips with a key idea, ideology, doctrine or concept by tapping into students' initial, spontaneous thoughts.

Aims

1. To stress the multi-faceted and subjective nature of key concepts.
2. To emphasize that key notions do not exist in a void.

What is needed

● Post-it notes.
● Felt-tip marker pens.
● A wall!

Time required

15 minutes.

How it works

The key idea under discussion is identified. Each student is given two Post-it notes and asked to write down two words or terms linked to the main idea. Each student in turn then places his or her stickers on the wall, and explains them as this is done. As

144

the wall is gradually covered, the students, or the tutor, can try to 'group together' similar ideas by creating clusters of Post-it notes on the wall. This creates a sense of the general group 'sentiment'.

A good example in action: Psychology – personality

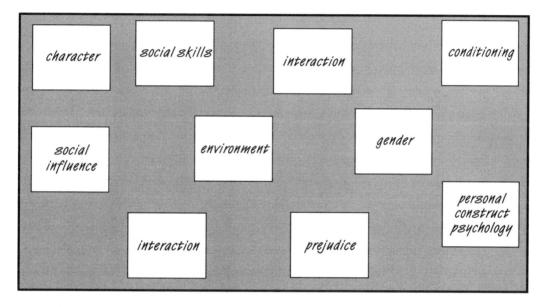

What debates would be stimulated by this Post-it wall?

Advantages of this activity

1.   It stimulates a potential variety of responses.
2.   It is very 'visual' – ideas are externalized.
3.   Everybody is involved – all opinions are valid.

Potential problem

Students must understand exactly what is required – the ground rules need to be clearly spelt out.

Main learning outcome

Students will gain an important awareness of how ideas and concepts are linked.

48

Theories as diagrams

In a nutshell

Theories (about anything) can initially be very difficult to grasp in abstract form and involve quite complex discussions. Hence there is a need to simplify, clarify and understand – but via non-verbal means. In this activity students attempt to represent their theory in graphic form. Discussion can then proceed about the set theory with everybody having a basic understanding or interest in the topic.

Aims

1. To make complex theories more accessible.
2. To acknowledge that some people learn best non-verbally – that is, by expressing ideas in a different, more creative and artistic form.

What is needed

- Felt-tip marker pens.
- A3 paper.
- Blu-tack.

Time required

10 minutes (turning the theory into a diagram) plus 10 minutes (follow-on discussion).

How it works

Students, in pairs, are asked to represent an important, and possibly complex, theory in graphic form. After ten minutes all the different diagrams are posted on the wall, and each pair explains their diagram in turn. Discussion can then commence on the different representations and the 'fundamental basics' of the theory.

A good example in action: Politics – separation of powers

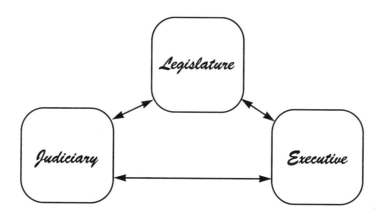

This is one student's attempt to represent 'separation of powers' in diagrammatic form. How is this image intended to clarify the concept? What do you think is the exact meaning and significance of the arrows? What problems are highlighted by this representation? How might other students try to represent the same concept? How could this particular diagram be enhanced? How would other people represent the concept?

Advantages of this activity

1. Complex theories are simplified and clarified.
2. Students are enfranchised via their own personal representations.
3. Students can appreciate the way in which other people might view the same theory.

Potential problems

Students may not understand enough to start trying to represent the theory in graphic form; also, some students lack confidence and creativity with felt-tips in hand!

Main learning outcome

The graphic representation, and the group discussion this fosters, will help the students to understand and analyse problematic theories.

49

3-D ideas

In a nutshell

Think about, and learn about, abstract concepts in a new and refreshing way by getting students to build, create, produce or mould a shape to represent the concept under consideration.

Aims

1. To think about ideas in a totally fresh manner.
2. To catalyse discussion around the central concept and the 'shapes' by which it is represented.
3. To make ideas more 'real' and 'accessible'.

What is needed

Lego, Plasticine or anything else that can be used to 'shape' an idea or a concept!!

Time required

15 minutes (shape creation) plus 10 minutes (discussion).

How it works

Students, either individually or in pairs, are given some kind of 'raw material', such as Lego or Plasticine, with which to shape the idea or concept under consideration.

The 3-D shapes are then used as a stimulus for discussion: why are certain shapes or moulds created to depict certain ideas and concepts?

A good example in action: Philosophy – democracy

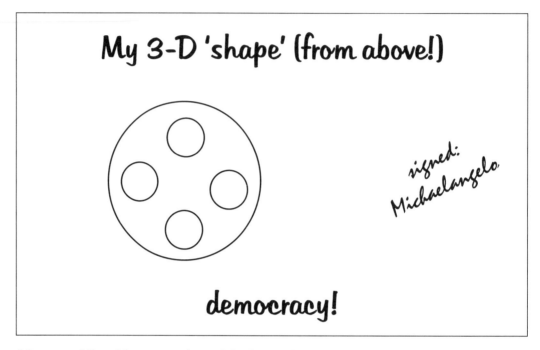

After moulding 'democracy' as a 3-D shape, the student then depicts the shape in a drawing: four equal small circles within a large circle. The obvious idea here is that democracy is about equality (four equal-sized circles) and about everyone having equal power and worth within a democracy (the big circle). But, is this the best, or only, way to represent democracy? How would other students think about the concept and represent it in 3-D form?

Advantages of this activity

1. It shows that practical means can be used to depict important ideas.
2. Although there might be no single common shape, there might be significant common 'threads' to discuss and analyse.
3. It challenges students – and provokes comment!
4. It is fun!

Potential problem

Students might view this hands-on, 3-D approach as 'childish' or 'not the kind of thing you do at college'.

Main learning outcomes

Students will gain a key insight into the subjectivity of ideas and concepts; they will also learn that ideas can be brought to life!

50

Opposites and enemies

In a nutshell

This is a card game in which students have to identify the 'opposites' and 'enemies' of certain abstract ideas.

Aims

1. To make abstract ideas more accessible and familiar.
2. To provoke students into thinking much more about the nature of selected ideas.

What is needed

*   Single cards with key ideas printed on them (to be prepared by the tutor beforehand).
*   Blank cards to be written on by students.

Time required

15 minutes (card game) plus 15 minutes (discussion).

How it works

The students are divided into subgroups, and each subgroup is given a card with an idea or concept printed on it. On five other cards they have to write down five ideas or concepts that oppose, or are contrary to, this concept or idea. Each group then passes on its five cards to another group for comment and analysis: in what sense are the five ideas contrary to the central idea or concept? Focused discussion can follow on in both the small- and whole-group contexts.

A good example in action: History of Ideas – nationalism

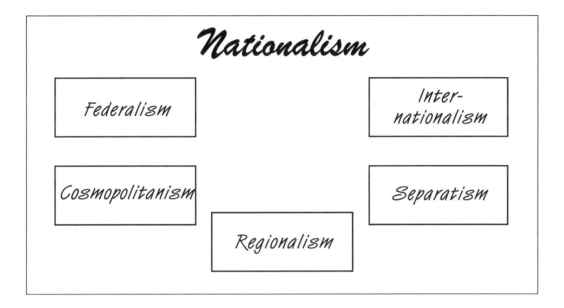

Advantages of this activity

1. Ideas are externalized on to pieces of card and are thus made more real and familiar.
2. It injects an element of competition and fun into classes, and the atmosphere can change for the better.

Potential problem

Students might be unsure about the 'rules' of the game – they need to be explained clearly!

Main learning outcomes

Students will gain an awareness and understanding of the relationship between important ideas and concepts. They will also be encouraged to discuss, and argue about, abstract ideas – particularly those which conflict or oppose each other.

51

Sub-ideas within a big idea

In a nutshell

This activity explores the make-up, the character and the nature of 'big' ideas. More specifically, the exercise seeks to promote understanding of important concepts by splitting them up into their component parts. Small student groups are asked to write out important 'sub-ideas' and 'sub-themes' on Post-it notes which are then displayed on the classroom wall for everyone to see and discuss.

Aims

1. To bring ideas alive – making them more 'real' by putting them up on the wall, so students can actually 'see' them and relate to them better.
2. To simplify and clarify key abstract concepts, and to emphasize the interrelationships evident between them.

What is needed

- Felt-tip marker pens.
- A pad of Post-it notes.

Time required

10 minutes (for students to write their sub-ideas on the Post-it notes) plus 20 minutes (for students to (a) introduce their sub-ideas to the class and (b) generate a plenary discussion).

How it works

Small student subgroups are given different abstract ideas to focus upon (one per group). They are also given five Post-it notes on which to write five different 'small' ideas – concepts or themes that together help explain the 'big' idea which they have been given. Each group then has to nominate one spokesperson, whose job it is to take the Post-it notes to the wall, stick them up and introduce them, and then – by moving the notes around – explain and elaborate on the relationships and interrelationships at play between the ideas and how they relate to the 'big idea'. Discussion and questions can then follow on.

A good example in action: Economics – monetarism

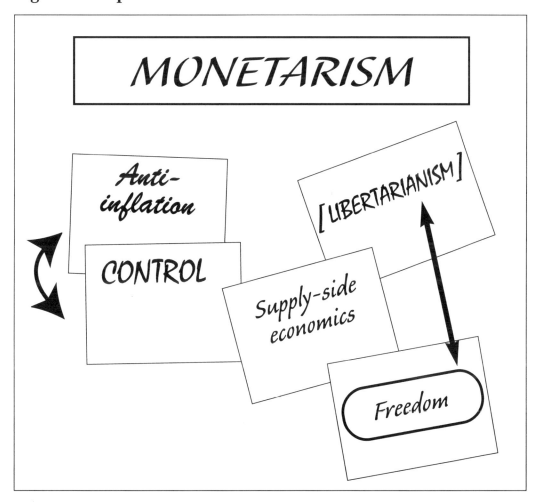

In the above diagram, the arrows show relationships between ideas. It is the task of the group's spokesperson to manipulate the notes on the wall to show the interplay, links and relationships between the concepts.

Any concept could be 'deconstructed' into its component 'small' ideas – conservatism, patriarchy, Keynesianism, and so on.

Advantages of this activity

1. It encourages students to think about the make-up of key concepts which are often just taken for granted.
2. It forces students to discuss and negotiate in small groups, and also to prioritize: for example, which are the five *most* important sub-ideas within the 'big' idea?
3. It enables students to manipulate ideas (on the wall) and demonstrate their conceptual dexterity, from which other students can understand and learn.

Potential problems

Students may write too much on their Post-it notes. The notes should only contain one or two words so that they are clear, simple and easy to read. Students also may not understand that they must not only stick their five 'sub-ideas' up on the wall but also manipulate them and show relationships – this must be emphasized!

Main learning outcome

Students will learn that ideas and concepts are accessible and are malleable, and that each idea or concept is related to, or actually incorporates, other sub-ideas.

52

Collage

In a nutshell

Bring life to an idea, concept or doctrine through a student-produced collage of images, pictures, words and headlines.

Aims

1. To foster the notion that ideas are accessible and that abstract concepts can be illustrated and illuminated with 'real-life' and 'everyday' images.
2. To catalyse discussion during and after the creation of the collage.

What is needed

*   A selection of old newspapers and glossy magazines.
*   A3/A2 paper.
*   Glue.
*   Scissors.
*   Blu-tack.

Time required

30 minutes (collage-making) plus 20 minutes (discussion).

How it works

Small subgroups are given one 'idea' to focus on (it may be the same idea, or each small group might be given a different idea to work on) plus a selection of old newspapers and glossy magazines with which to create a collage. Pictures, images, headlines or just words can be culled to produce a collage on the set theme. Each subgroup displays their collage on the wall and then introduces and explains their montage and its make-up. As this process takes place, questions can be addressed to the group and, after all the subgroups have explained their collages, a whole-group discussion can follow.

A good example in action: Sociology – patriarchy

This is one student-produced collage. Why did this group pick these images? What type of discussion would the photographs and words provoke?

Advantages of this activity

1. It's practical – but discussion and conversation can accompany all the 'doing', 'cutting' and 'pasting'.
2. Ideas can be illuminated superbly by recourse to images, photographs, words and so on.

Potential problem

Students might resist the idea – it's unusual, practical and probably not what they expect from college classes.

Main learning outcomes

Students will understand that any concept can be represented and articulated in graphic form; they will also be drawn into debate about why certain images were chosen, and into the more general debate about the real nature and meaning of the abstract idea under consideration.

Summary and evaluation

On the whole, students view abstract ideas – and the art of conceptualizing about abstract ideas – as 'alien'. Experience shows that students are frightened of ideas; they prefer more 'concrete' topics – events, personalities and the like. To make abstract ideas more accessible for students is, therefore, an important and an urgent task, and one that this chapter has tried to address.

Several principles have emerged. First, it is usually a beneficial tactic to simplify abstract ideas and then, in time, build upon this solid base. Second, there are definite merits in 'externalizing' ideas – by writing them down or making them the subject of a role-play or another type of creative exercise. This can make ideas more 'familiar' and more interesting. Third, and in a very general sense, concepts need to be brought alive – and most of the activities described in this chapter do attempt to enliven and illuminate ideas. In some cases, this might mean 'attacking' ideas from new and perhaps controversial perspectives, such as pictorial representation, drawing or 3-D modelling.

Undoubtedly though, the 'purists' and 'traditionalists' will raise an eyebrow at such techniques. Equally, however, many observers – and, more significantly, many practitioners – are convinced that abstract concepts can be expressed in non-verbal form and that pictorial representation can be an entirely legitimate 'way-in' to the consideration and discussion of abstract ideas and theories. Methods like this are perhaps particularly helpful for less academically gifted students – surely a key attribute. Conceptualization is a very difficult skill to acquire, and some students may need a 'helping hand' in this context.

Ideas can also be 'active', and card games, Post-it walls and all manner of other activities can be employed to bring ideas 'alive' and make them more interesting and enjoyable. Teaching abstract ideas is a considerable challenge and, if the key aim is to catalyse and stimulate meaningful classroom discussion, no means should be overlooked or disregarded.

7 Primary documents

With key texts, like the Good Samaritan for example, the aim is always to get inside the text and unravel it. You could invent as many characters as you want – and the people in the group would be asked to act out their character. A discussion would then follow about the scenario under consideration.
Rev. Inderjit Bhogal, Urban Theology Unit, Sheffield

Introduction

One constant dimension to teaching in the humanities and social sciences is the emphasis on significant texts – whether these be key phrases or quotations, whole documents, charters or manifestos. In certain situations students may be able to familiarize themselves with the texts prior to the class session but, for the most part, this cannot be guaranteed!

This means that, sometimes, tutors might be forced to discuss the text in class. On other occasions they might even want to introduce the text to a class suddenly – and surprise and shock them in the process! Either way, the tutor has to find a workable strategy to bring the session alive and to get the best out of a text (which might be rather dull).

This chapter, therefore, contains a selection of workable and imaginative primary document 'activities'. I would like to thank Maggie Sheen, Rowland Goodwin, Sue Havens and Val Bryson for their ideas for this chapter.

Related activities

The following activities, outlined and explained in other chapters, also include an important 'primary text' element:

53

Text and context

In a nutshell

A set passage is under consideration. The tutor splits up the group in an attempt to analyse and explore the text more thoroughly, with each subgroup given specific areas and questions to assess.

Aims

1. To set important texts in context and to understand the true nature and meaning of key extracts.
2. To prepare students for answering document/extract questions.

What is needed

- Copies of the set passage.
- A3 paper.
- Felt-tip marker pens.

Time required

10 minutes (small-group discussion) plus 20 minutes (explanation of poster ideas and general discussion).

How it works

The tutor introduces the exercise and, with the whole group, looks over and familiarizes themselves with the key text. The students are then split into subgroups of three or four, with each subgroup discussing and evaluating one 'angle' on the text – for example:

● Why the text was written.
● The nature and tone of the text.
● The 'implications' and 'consequences' of the text.

Each subgroup then writes up its conclusions on an A3 wall poster. The tutor reconvenes the whole group, and each subgroup reports on its findings to the group using its poster. Discussion ensues on the contextual issues surrounding the set passage.

A good example in action: English – *Shame*

The turning door-knob rattles like a drum. At once there is a change in the quality of the night. A delicious wickedness is in the air. A cool breeze stirs, as if the entry of the first man has succeeded in dispelling some of the intense treacly heat of the hot season, enabling the ceiling fans to move a little more efficiently through the soupy atmosphere... (Rushdie, p.72)

● Subgroup A: What is the background to this passage?
● Subgroup B: What is the nature and tone of the passage?
● Subgroup C: What is the significance and consequence of this passage?

Advantages of this activity

1. Students are able to discuss their thoughts in small buzz groups.
2. The full meaning of the text emerges from all three groups' deliberations.
3. The key text is analysed very thoroughly, and not just skirted over.

Potential problems

Students may not understand some words in the text – the tutor should pre-empt any difficulties! There may also be a problem of overlap: the three groups should emerge with quite distinct ideas and not tread on each other's territory!

Main learning outcomes

Students will acquire an important awareness of contextualization – an understanding of the different influences on, and consequences of, a certain text – and also an improved ability to tackle document/extract commentaries.

54

Quotation deconstruction

In a nutshell

Institute a thorough and in-depth analysis of a key quotation or short passage by copying the quote onto a large wall poster and then deconstructing it.

Aims

1. To illustrate the construction of, and nuances within, a key quote or passage.
2. To increase students' critical awareness of words, themes and meanings.

What is needed

- A very large sheet of paper to act as a wall poster.
- Blu-tack.
- Felt-tip marker pens.

Time required

15 minutes (whole-group discussion).

How it works

The key quotation/passage is written, using a felt-tip marker pen, on a massive wall poster and fixed to the classroom wall. The class begins to analyse the language and vocabulary in the passage, with students in turn denoting and marking the significant words with the pen. By the end of the class, the quotation should have been thoroughly dissected, with discussion ensuing as each aspect of it is noted and considered.

A good example in action: RE – John Wesley

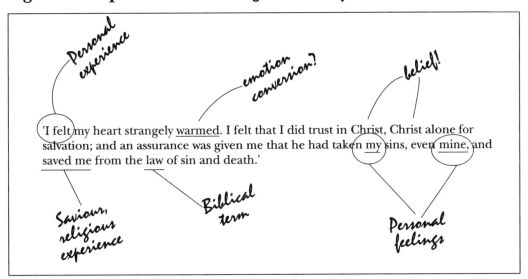

Source: Plumb, 1966, p.92.

This quote is written up on a poster in big letters, and fixed to the wall. Students, in turn, mark the key textual points (as above).

Advantages of this activity

1. Students will gain the ability to scrutinize and analyse a key passage.
2. There is a beneficial 'visual' dimension – all the students can see the quote and the markings.
3. All students are encouraged to take part.

Potential problem

When several students have marked the poster, it might begin to look a little untidy – students must keep their contributions neat!

Main learning outcome

Students will be helped to think about key quotations that appear in essay questions, and also short passages that often form the basis of document/extract commentaries.

55

Newspaper headlines

In a nutshell

This activity is all about texts – and the 'newspaper headlines' they warrant and deserve.

Aims

1. To concentrate students' minds on the content of important texts.
2. To make students think about the salient and keynote features of significant passages.

What is needed

● A set of key newspaper passages with their headlines removed.
● A4 paper.
● Felt-tip marker pens.
● Blu-tack.

Time required

15 minutes (small-group work on headlines) plus 10 minutes (whole-group discussion).

How it works

Small student subgroups are given a selection of key newspaper reports, with their

166

headlines removed, to study and, ultimately, 'headline'. The students read the passages, evaluate the main issues involved and designate an effective, pertinent headline for each story. They then write these headlines on blank pieces of paper and stick these up on the wall for the whole class to see. The tutor then chairs a discussion about the headlines, the reports and the way in which the new headlines capture (or do not capture!) the essence of the stories.

A good example in action: Law – 1994 case

What headline should accompany the following report? Why?

Regina v Winston Brown.
Court of Appeal (Criminal Division) (Lord Justice Steyn, Mr Justice Owen and Mr Justice Ian Kennedy).
15 June 1994.
The prosecution is not under a legal duty to disclose to the defence material which is only relevant to the credibility of defence witnesses.
The Court of Appeal dismissed the appellant's appeal against conviction of wounding with intent to do grievous bodily harm.

The defendant's alibi to the Crown's allegation that he had stabbed the victim was supported by two witnesses. In cross-examination, one witness admitted he may have told the police that he was too drunk to recall the defendant's whereabouts and the other said he had withdrawn his statement to the police implicating the defendant because of threats.

The defendant appealed on the ground that the Crown owed a duty to disclose information which tended to reflect on the honesty of defence witnesses.
Ian McMeekin (Registrar of Criminal Appeals) for the appellant; *Alan Conrad (CPS)* for the Crown.
LORD JUSTICE STEYN, giving the court's judgment, said that the Attorney-General's Guidelines (1981) 74 Cr App R 302 were merely a set of instructions to Crown Prosecution Service lawyers and prosecution counsel. They did not have the force of law.

Today the guidelines did not conform to the requirements of the law of disclosure in a number of critically important respects. First, it was for the court, not prosecuting counsel, to decide on disputed questions as to disclosable materials and on any asserted legal ground to withhold production of relevant material. The procedure to be adopted, whether *inter partes* or exceptionally *ex parte*, was governed by rules of practice laid down in *R v Davis [1993] 1 WLR 613; R v Keane [1994] 1 WLR 746* and *R v Johnson*, unreported, 15 January 1993.

There was no hint in the guidelines of the primacy of the court in deciding on issues of disclosure. The guidelines were not an exhaustive statement of the Crown's common law duty of disclosure. The guidelines were drafted before major developments in the field of public interest immunity.

The divergences between the guidelines and the common law showed the value of the guidelines as a set of instructions to prosecutors had largely been eroded by major legal developments. It was in the public interest that that reality should be addressed.

It was to the common law that the criminal justice system must turn to provide the framework of rules which governed disclosure by the Crown. The objective of the criminal justice system was the control of crime. It was axiomatic that everybody who came before our courts was entitled to a fair trial.

In our adversarial sustem, in which the police and prosecution controlled the investigatory process, an accused's right to fair disclosure was an inseparable part of his right to a fair trial.

In a criminal case, the Crown was under a duty to give disclosure of significant material which might affect the credibility of a prosecution witness. The Crown was therefore obliged to disclose previous statements of prosecution witnesses and to disclose previous convictions of a prosecution witness. The duty of disclosure applied equally to written and oral statements.

The law on public interest immunity in criminal proceedings was not yet fully developed. However, four propositions were now clearly established. It was for the court rule on the question of immunity and that necessarily involved the court studying the material for which immunity was claimed. The judge must always perform a balancing exercise, taking into account the public interest and the interests of the defendant. If the disputed material might prove the defendant's innocence or avoid a miscarriage of justice, then the balance came down resoundingly in favour of disclosing it. Even if the trial judge initially decided against disclosure he was under a continuous duty, in the light of the way in which the trial developed, to keep that decision under review.

Prosecuting counsel must inform himself fully about the content of any disputed material so that he was in a position to invite the judge to re-assess the situation if the previous denial of the material arguably became untenable in the light of developments in the trial.

Turning to the appeal, it was axiomatic that the duty to disclose extended to material which might arguably undermine the prosecution case or assist a defendant's case. In current practice, the Crown disclosed the previous convictions of the defendant but not the previous convictions of defence witnesses.

There must be a limit to the scope of discovery that could be required of the Crown. A defendant's solicitor was in a position to inquire from a defence witness or others about his past or about other matters affecting his credibility. It would impose an unnecessary and excessive burden on the Crown to impose a legal duty to disclose material which was only relevant to the credibility of defence witnesses. The submission that the Crown was under a legal duty to disclose previous convictions of defence witnesses was rejected.
Ying Hui Tan, Barrister

Source: The Independent, 22 June 1994.

What should a good headline do? What main themes emerge from the students' efforts? What is the relationship between the headlines and the report? How might this exercise provoke discussion?

Real headline

Disclosure guidelines' value eroded

Advantages of this activity

1. It asks students for clarity.
2. It compels students to prioritize – what is the real story?
3. It encourages students to read the texts thoroughly, analyse them coherently, and evaluate them succinctly.
4. The headlines, once mounted on the wall, can stimulate further discussion.

Potential problem

Students may find it extremely difficult to summarize the reports concisely, but that is the crux of the exercise!

Main learning outcome

Students will be exposed to a series of newspaper reports – a key type of source – and will use their judgement to summarize the passages and justify their decisions.

Variations

1. Why not reverse the exercise – and ask students to write the report, not the headline? Give the students a set of headlines and ask them, in pairs, to write a newspaper-style report to fit the headline.
2. When students are studying a significant event or development, why not ask them to write newspaper reports on it – but from different political or ideological perspectives? How about a right-wing view on a particularly crucial incident in the 1984 miners' strike or a left-wing view on Mussolini's March on Rome?
3. Ask students to compare and contrast different newspapers' accounts of the same event, pinpointing key words which illustrate bias.
4. To uncover the real truth, ask the students to distinguish between 'fact' and 'opinion' within newspaper reports. Ask them to erase all 'opinions' from a report and then write about the 'facts' from a different perspective.

56

Create a charter!

In a nutshell

Combat the possible boredom and dullness of combing through a 'real-life' charter or official document by keeping the real text hidden and asking students to create their own document, basing their efforts on their own innate background knowledge and their own insights into what has gone wrong with the real one.

Aims

1. To illuminate the 'process' involved in the writing of official documents, including the problems and difficulties.
2. To enable students to compare and contrast 'real' and 'student-written' texts.

What is needed

● A3 paper.
● Felt-tip marker pens.
● Blu-tack.

Time required

30 minutes (charter writing) plus 20 minutes (class discussion).

How it works

Having outlined the principles upon which a key charter was constructed in a

169

previous session (and without revealing the 'real' text), the tutor asks the students to write their 'imaginary', 'ultimate' or 'Utopian' charters. The students undertake this task in pairs and write up their document on an A3 poster for the whole class to see. With several would-be 'charters' on the wall, comparisons and contrasts can be made. At the end of the class the real document is unwrapped and a constructive discussion can follow.

A good example in action: Politics – the US Constitution

OUR **NEW**
NATION IS PROUD
TO PROCLAIM . . .

I. CITIZENS HAVE
<u>RIGHTS</u> AND <u>DUTIES</u>

* * *

II. THE PRESIDENT
SHALL REPRESENT
AND EMBODY THE
STATE . . .

A POSSIBLE EXCERPT FROM A STUDENT-WRITTEN CHARTER

Advantages of this activity

1. Students are introduced to the problems and complexities involved in real-life charter-making.
2. It is a creative, rather than passive, exercise.
3. The range of different student ideas should provoke an excellent discussion about the fundamentals of certain official documents, and also encourage students to prioritize ideas and understand national political cultures.

Potential problem

Students might think that there is a 'right answer', and this might impede their early efforts.

Main learning outcome

Students will become involved in the process of converting fundamental principles into real-life practical articles.

57

Read out loud!

In a nutshell

Bring a text to life by going round the group and asking each student in turn to read out a sentence, and asking another student to spontaneously analyse and interpret.

Aims

1. To involve all the students in the rigorous analysis of a set passage.
2. To provide a comprehensive and intricate step-by-step review of the text.

What is needed

Copies of the set text.

Time required

This obviously depends on the length of the text but, ideally, an exercise such as this should last no more than 20 minutes plus 10 minutes for a general discussion on the passage at the end.

How it works

Students sit in a circle, each with a copy of the set passage. Student A reads out loud the first line of the passage; Student B, Student A's neighbour to the left, provides a 30-second commentary on the sentence that has just been read out. Student C (to the left of Student B) then reads out the next sentence, and Student D interprets. This procedure continues until the whole passage, or a selected portion of it, is completed. Discussion can then ensue about the main themes and the general importance of the passage.

A good example in action: English – Dickens, *Great Expectations*

Student A (reading line 1 from *Great Expectations*): *My father's family name being Pirrip, and my christian name Philip, my infant tongue could make of both names nothing longer or more explicit than Pip.*
Student B (interpreting line 1): 'Well, I think the significance of this line is that … As the first line in the whole novel, it …'
Student C (reading line 2 from the book): *So, I called myself Pip, and came to be called Pip.*
Student D (interpreting line 2): 'This is a very short sentence, and because of this it's very striking. I think Dickens is trying to …'
Student E (reading line 3 from the book): *I gave Pirrip as my father's family name, on the authority of his tombstone and my sister – Mrs. Joe Gargery, who married the blacksmith.*
Student F (interpreting line 3): 'I don't quite understand the significance of this line. Is Dickens just gradually outlining the context of things and introducing the key characters? Has anyone else got any thoughts?'

And so on …

Advantages of this activity

1. All the students feel involved, and know that they each have a key role to play.
2. By the end of the passage – and after each individual interpretation – the passage will have been considered and thoroughly analysed.

Potential problems

Some students may be inarticulate and unfocused as 'interpreters' – other more incisive students can be brought in at this point! Quiet students might find the whole exercise difficult but, hopefully, they will be able to develop their communication skills during the session.

Main learning outcome

The passage is analysed in increments and in the whole: students' understanding is increased and their technique for answering documentary extract questions is improved.

58

Paragraphs

In a nutshell

Split an important and perhaps fairly long passage into paragraphs, to make the text more manageable, and ask pairs of students to provide a comprehensive, clear interpretation of each paragraph.

Aims

1. To involve all the students in the decoding and analysis of a key text.
2. To show that all parts of a text – even the most unassuming – have key meanings and can all help in acquiring an understanding of the passage as a whole.

What is needed

- Copies of the key text.
- A3 paper.
- Felt-tip pens.
- Blu-tack.

Time required

10 minutes (pairwork on paragraphs) plus 15 minutes (whole-group discussion).

How it works

Students are paired up and the text is divided into paragraphs. Each pair gets a paragraph to analyse, and are asked to pick out two key words and two key themes. The students write these words and themes up on to an A3 poster and, in turn, the pairs go to their poster and introduce and explain their words. After each pair has done this, the whole text has, effectively, been explained and further discussion in the whole group can take place.

A good example in action: History – the Truman Doctrine (1947)

Paragraph 1: *At the present moment in world history nearly every nation must choose between alternative ways of life. The choice is too often not a free one.*

Student pair no. 1:
Words: 'choice' and 'alternative'.
Themes:
1. 'The world is at a crucial turning-point'.
2. 'Freedom v. dictatorship'.
(The pair of students would explain and elaborate upon the words and themes)

Paragraph 2: *One way of life is based upon the will of the majority, and is distinguished by free institutions, representative government, free elections, guarantees of individual liberty, freedom of speech and religion, and freedom from political oppression.*

Student pair no. 2
Words: 'majority' and 'freedom'.
Themes:
1. 'The world is divided'.
2. 'Democracy is the "good" and "better" system'.

Paragraph 3: *The second way of life is based upon the will of a minority forcibly imposed upon the majority. It relies upon terror and oppression, a controlled press and radio, fixed elections, and the suppression of personal freedoms.*

Student pair no. 3
Words: 'minority' and 'terror'.
Themes:
1. 'Dictatorship does rule in some countries'.
2. 'Dictatorship is "bad" and relies on terror'.
And so on...
Source: Lane, 1985, pp. 60, 77–8.

Advantages of this activity

1. Students benefit from other students' work.
2. The whole passage is analysed in an ordered manner.

Potential problem

Students might be given a difficult paragraph to analyse and might have to delve into other paragraphs to find out important contextual information.

Main learning outcome

Students will be exposed to a key paragraph of text and will incisively identify the crucial words and themes.

59

Role-play a text

In a nutshell

Analyse a text through role-play. Pick out the key characters, allocate a key character to each student subgroup, and then structure the group discussion around the characters and their roles and motivations in the text.

Aims

1. To bring texts alive.
2. To involve all students, actively, in the explanation and analysis of a text.

What is needed

Copies of the set text – one per student.

Time required

10 minutes (small-group discussion and role-play) plus 15 minutes (whole-group discussion).

How it works

The set text is unveiled, and the identities of the key characters are determined and discussed. Each figure in the text is 'given' to a small student subgroup which then thinks about, and analyses, the significant characteristics of 'their' person, and how their character is involved in the text, including the nature of involvement, its underlying motivations and consequences. The tutor then chairs a discussion about the passage, with one person in each group speaking as, and on behalf of, his or her group's character.

A good example in action: RE – Jesus heals a crippled woman on the Sabbath

One Sabbath Jesus was teaching in a synagogue. A woman there had an evil spirit that had made her ill for eighteen years; she was bent over and could not straighten up at all. When Jesus saw her, he called out to her, 'Woman, you are free from your illness!' He placed his hands on her, and at once she straightened herself up and praised God.

The official of the synagogue was angry that Jesus had healed on the Sabbath, so he spoke up and said to the people, 'There are six days in which we should work; so come during those days and be healed, but not on the Sabbath!'

The Lord answered him, 'You hypocrites! Any one of you would untie his ox or his donkey from the stall and take it out to give it water on the Sabbath. Now here is this descendant of Abraham whom Satan has kept bound up for eighteen years; should she not be released on the Sabbath?' His answer made his enemies ashamed of themselves, while the people rejoiced over all the wonderful things that he did.
Luke 13:10–17, *Good News Bible*, 1987, p.98

The role-play subgroups are:

- Jesus
- Woman in the synagogue
- Synagogue official.

The questions to be considered in the small-group phase are:

1. How do these people and groups feel about their role and involvement in the text?
2. How are they portrayed and depicted in the document?
3. What are the relationships at play in the text?

Advantages of this activity

1. Complex or dull texts can be enlivened and made more interesting.
2. All the students are actively involved in the exercise.

Potential problem

Some allocated roles may be quite minor, and some students may feel slightly 'excluded'.

Main learning outcomes

Students will increase their understanding of the nature and nuances of a set text and will empathize with, and explore the character of, one key protagonist in the text.

Variations

1. An element of drama can also be introduced, with each group designating one member to 'act out' or 'sculpt' their character, thus giving the group session an added energy.
2. A 'press' element can be introduced: certain members of the tutor group can be asked to play journalists and to devise questions which they would like to ask the role-play characters after reading through the text. The role-play characters then have to improvise answers.

60

Predict the passage

In a nutshell

Instead of just handing students a key text or passage or speech, set the background and context and ask students to actually write it.

Aims

1. To put students into the mindset of key individuals or organizations.
2. To foster students' awareness of the conditioning factors that affect the writing of key documents.

What is needed

Paper and pens.

Time required

30 minutes (passage-writing) plus 10 minutes (for passages to be read out) plus 10 minutes (for general plenary discussion).

How it works

The tutor outlines the key background information – in particular, the authorship and context of the passage. The students, in pairs, are then given 30 minutes to think about, discuss and actually 'write' the passage. During this period, students will discuss and consider the important details – the nature of the document, the motivations that lie behind it, and its possible ramifications or implications. Each pair then reads out their effort. This is followed by a whole-group discussion on differences between the passages produced by the various student subgroups, and also how the student efforts compare to the real text.

A good example in action: Media Studies – PCC Code of Practice on 'Intrusions into grief or shock'

The following statements are the efforts of the different student groups:

1. 'Journalists have a responsibility to carry out their duties with due regard for the personal feelings of individuals involved in the news.'
2. 'Journalists should try to maintain high moral standards in all their dealings with the general public.'
3. 'It is the duty of journalists to behave respectfully towards all individuals they come into contact with.'

The actual statement is as follows:

In cases involving personal grief or shock, enquiries should be carried out and approaches made with sympathy and discretion. (Keeble, 1990, p.352)

How close are the student efforts? What are the main themes to emerge from them? What questions are raised by this exercise?

Advantages of this activity

1. Students spend the whole session, in one form or another, discussing the text.
2. It is far more interesting and imaginative than just reading over the actual speech.

Potential problem

Students may find it very challenging to enter another's mindset and write, convincingly and constructively, from this perspective.

Main learning outcomes

Students will gain a key insight into the process of drafting key texts and will also be encouraged to empathize, imagine and speculate in an intelligent manner.

61

Maximum three

In a nutshell

Simplify and clarify a codified charter, constitution or manifesto by abbreviating its contents into 'short and snappy' summary points (three words maximum).

Aims

1. To increase understanding of a key document.
2. To cut through the complex jargon so often associated with official texts.

What is needed

- Copies of the set charter, constitution or manifesto.
- A3 paper.
- Felt-tip marker pens.
- Blu-tack.

Time required

10 minutes (work in subgroups) plus 10 minutes (whole-group discussion).

How it works

If the charter, manifesto or constitution has, for example, 12 points, the group is split into four subgroups, with each group responsible for three points each. Each subgroup has to read, understand and abbreviate each of their points into a simple but illuminating (and perhaps even humorous!) three-word summary. Each group writes its abbreviated points onto separate sheets of A4 paper. In turn, each group is asked to explain its thinking on the points it was given.

Within 10 minutes, the whole document is summarized (twice – each group might have a different perspective on the document). All the students can take advantage of their colleagues' work in simplifying the other terms/articles by writing down the whole document in condensed form, and using this as a record of the session. A whole-group discussion about the exercise – and its results – can then take place.

A good example in action: Media Studies – NUJ Code of Conduct

1. *A journalist has a duty to maintain the highest professional and ethical standards.*
2. *A journalist shall at all times defend the principle of the freedom of the press and other media in relation to the collection of information and the expression of comment and criticism. He/she shall strive to eliminate distortion, news suppression and censorship.*
3. *A journalist shall strive to ensure that the information he/she disseminates is fair and accurate, avoid the expression of comment and conjecture as established fact and falsification by distortion, selection or misrepresentation.*
    Keeble, 1990, p.349

Point 1   **Must be honest** *(Group A)*

Point 2   **Press freedom vital** *(Group B)*

Point 3   **No exaggeration/speculation** *(Group C)*

Advantages of this activity

1. Students will share their knowledge and summary for the benefit of the group.
2. Simplifying complex ideas is an impressive skill, and can lead to a better general understanding of the whole document.

Potential problem

Students may opt for 'jokey' three-word responses rather than more incisive, 'spot-on' answers.

Main learning outcome

Students will understand that complex documents can be made more accessible, and that abbreviated summaries can only follow on from good, general understanding.

62

Key words

In a nutshell

Analyse the importance of a key text, diary entry or memoir by asking small student subgroups to identify what they think are the three most important, poignant or powerful words in the passage.

Aims

1. To increase students' powers of documentary analysis.
2. To encourage students to pinpoint, and then explain, the significance and importance of key words in a set passage.

What is needed

- Copies of the key text.
- Post-it notes.
- Felt-tip marker pens.

Time required

10 minutes (groupwork) plus 15 minutes (whole-group discussion).

How it works

Groups of four students are given an identical text. They are asked to write out the three most poignant or important words (or short phrases) on separate Post-it notes. Each group elects a spokesperson who, in turn, attaches his or her group's stickers to the wall, not randomly but with an awareness of how their words relate to those already displayed. In this way, small clusters indicating the most popular words or themes and overlaps are formed. This exercise is followed by a whole-group discussion.

A good example in action: Psychology – theories of personality

When we consider a person's life-history, we see that sometimes his fate is determined more by the objects which attract his interest, while sometimes it is influenced rather by his own inner, subjective states.... Quite generally one might characterize the introverted *point of view by pointing to the constant subjection of the object and objective reality to the ego and the subjective psychological processes.... According to the* extraverted *point of view, the* subject *is considered as inferior to the object; the importance of the subjective aspect is only secondary.*
Carl Jung, quoted in Eysenck, 1953, p.23

The following words were picked out by one student group:

- 'introverted'
- 'extraverted'
- 'subject'

Are these the key words? Why are they important and significant? How do they relate to each other? And to other words picked out by other groups?

Advantages of this activity

1. The array, and clusters, of Post-it notes on the wall will indicate the general opinions of the group as to the most important words and themes in the passage, and this will act as an interesting catalyst to discussion.
2. It has two refreshing dimensions – students have to stand up and move around to display their stickers; they also have to 'study' the wall to draw conclusions and evaluate relationships.

Potential problem

Students may pick out fairly long phrases, and the clarity of the wall display could be adversely affected.

Main learning outcome

Students will have to concentrate on a key passage and be inducted into skills very relevant to answering documentary analysis questions.

Summary and evaluation

Humanities and social science subjects revolve around texts: poems, extracts from key texts and speeches, government documents, diary memoirs, eye-witness reports, newspaper editorials and the like. Short, snappy and meaningful texts make excellent 'raw material' for class sessions, but tutors may be a little predictable in the way they think about texts – for example, saying, 'Right, here's a short extract from Churchill's speech. Read it through and let me know what you make of it'.

Texts can certainly be used as brilliant small-group stimuli, but surely we have to be much more imaginative, creative and inventive in the way we attempt to exploit them?

In this vein it is interesting to pick up on the ideas of Sunday school teachers and church ministers. With small children, and with grown adults, the challenge for these groupwork practitioners is to bring Biblical texts alive. 'Creative Bible Study' is a recent development, and the more progressive ministers are now using such strategies as role-play to encourage their congregations to think about key passages from the Bible.

Role-play, however, is just one method. Another key principle is to actually withhold the central text, and instead use all manner of means to get students to consider what the nature of the key passage might be, could be, or even should be. With such 'predictive' methods there is instant discussion, and also the added ingredient of rivalry and competition between students.

Thus, texts can be role-played, predicted, simplified, deconstructed or merely read out loud! Students have all the time in the world to read and reread key texts outside class, so why not make the most of texts inside the classroom by spicing them up and adding just a touch of make-believe?

8 Numerical Data

With statistics I think you can be imaginative and you can make them interesting!
Dr John Fazey, Staff Development, University College Bangor

Introduction

Tutors in the humanities and social sciences regularly refer to numerical data for examples or illustrative purposes. Statistical tables can often reveal vital information and important evidence – evidence that, ultimately, can become crucial in the context of academic debate. 'Numbers', however, can be notoriously difficult to teach. For students they are often troublesome. They can also have the effect of intimidating and boring students. So, what can be done?

The contention of this chapter is that, with a little imagination and ingenuity, numerical and tabular data can definitely be brought to life, made more interesting and, yes, even exciting! With this in mind, a selection of activities, which all aim to catalyse discussion around numbers and statistical tables, will be introduced and explained – and each, obviously, can be altered to specific teaching needs. From role-play and posters to puzzles and games, there are a plethora of ways to make numerical data interesting and accessible.

I am deeply indebted to John Fazey (Staff Development, University College Bangor) for his huge input into this chapter. I was very fortunate to be able to meet John in Bangor, and to interview him at length. Many of the activities included in this chapter stem from this interview, and the stimulating exchange of ideas that this incorporated. John outlined to me eight principles that underpin the art of game creation in the specific context of tables and numerical data. At this juncture it would be entirely apt to cite these principles in full:

1. **Variation**: trying to present and analyse numerical data in a diverse and varied manner.

2. **Turning numbers 'on their head'**: looking at things from different or reverse perspectives.

3. **Taking numbers or other variables 'out'**: erasing key pieces of information from data tables in an effort to challenge and provoke students.

4. **Getting students to do what the tutor usually does**: perhaps asking students to invent a classroom strategy for dealing with numbers or actually to take over the tutor's role in the class.

5. **Making comparisons**: thinking about the way in which certain pieces of data relate to, and perhaps contrast with, other pieces of data.

6. **Putting numbers 'in'**: changing and doctoring data in an effort to catalyse discussion.

7. **Including numbers that are 'bogus', 'wrong' or 'false'**: challenging students to identify, and then explain, why certain pieces of data look out of place.

8. **Extrapolation**: asking students to think through the consequences, implications or ramifications of certain pieces of data.

I hope the activities contained in this chapter build upon these principles, and also upon John's expertise and enthusiasm. I would also like to thank Christine Bell and Derek Lynch for their suggestions.

Related activities

The following activities, outlined and explained in other chapters, also include an important 'statistical' or 'tabular' element:

63

Socio-economic predictions

In a nutshell

Instead of giving statistics to students – whether opinion poll data or electoral details – why not keep the figures secret and ask them to predict the exact figures on the basis of their insights and knowledge and introduce an element of role-play too?

Aims

1. To investigate and illuminate important electoral data from a different perspective.
2. To introduce an element of role-play and excitement into an area of study – numbers and tables – that is usually taught in a very dry and predictable manner.

What is needed

●   Small pieces of card, each marked with a 'group identity'.
●   Small pieces of card, denoting background information.
●   Sheets of A4 paper.
●   Felt-tip marker pens.
●   Blu-tack.

Time required

10 minutes (discussion and predictions in small groups) plus 15 minutes (unveiling of 'real' statistics and further discussion).

How it works

A key opinion poll or piece of electoral data is introduced, but the actual results are not revealed. The students are split into small groups and each group is given a card denoting a 'group identity' – for example, 'workers', 'employers', 'farmers', 'top executives', 'unemployed', or 'pensioners'. In their groups the students have to predict the level of support that 'their' group of people would give to whatever the question is (if the data under consideration is an opinion poll), or to the named political parties (if it is an election result that is under the spotlight). To help in this respect, the tutor gives each group a small selection of cards bearing miscellaneous information (each piece of information written on a separate piece of card). Some of the information might be helpful and directly relevant (on, say, social trends, economic indicators, historical patterns and so on). Other cards may be 'red herrings'! Some groups might have no real helpful information – and thus these students might have to make really bold predictions!

After 10 minutes of group discussion, each group predicts a figure, based on their accumulated knowledge, their discussion in the subgroup and the background material supplied. The students have to make informed estimates, and explain why they – as farmers or workers, for example – think or vote as they do. They write their group identity and their percentage opinion or 'vote' (for each party) on an A4 piece of paper and then attach these to the wall. The tutor reveals the 'real' data, and leads a discussion on the accuracy (or inaccuracy) of the predictions. What is surprising about the real figures? Why are the figures surprising?

If the real statistics are revealed halfway through a class, the session takes on a nice symmetry: making predictions in the first half and analysing them in the second half.

A good example in action: Politics – British politics and the pensioners' vote

GROUP B: WE ARE:

'*PENSIONERS*'

	WE PREDICT	REAL FIGURES
CONS	24%	36%
LAB	84%	55%
LIB DEM	12%	9%

Advantages of this activity

1. To make accurate predictions students have to focus, discuss and use their accumulated knowledge and insights.
2. It has an element of healthy competition between the student subgroups and the tutor (who is concealing the real figures).
3. It is an alternative to the traditional ways of discussing numbers and tables.

Potential problem

Students are naturally 'scared' of statistics, so they should be eased into this new way of studying them.

Main learning outcomes

Students will consider the viewpoint of a specific group of voters, and will be compelled to understand and empathize with their particular political perspective. They will also have to judge the worth of the miscellaneous facts and indicators given to them by the tutor.

64

Recognition tests

In a nutshell

Vary the usual approach to statistics by 'blanking out' the categories on one axis in a table (but leaving the axis title intact). Ask students, on the evidence of the figures in the table and on the basis of their general knowledge of the subject, to make informed predictions about the axis categories which have been erased. In essence this is a 'recognition test': students are challenged to identify the axis categories on the evidence of the figures in the tables.

What is needed

Copies of the tables, with the categories on one axis blanked out.

Time required

15 minutes (small-group discussion) plus 15 minutes (whole-group discussion).

How it works

Small groups of two or three students are given key statistical tables with the categories on one axis blanked out. On the basis of what they already know, the students have to fill in the missing categories on the axis in question. The tutor eventually reveals the correct axis categories, and then leads a discussion on the principal issues raised.

A good example in action: Sociology – causes of poverty (1950–60)

Cause of poverty	% of those in poverty (Rowntree 1950)	% of those in poverty (Abel-Smith & Townsend 1960)
a	4	40
b	68	33
c	7	10
d	21	10
e	0	7

Category options: Sickness; Old age; Unemployment; Inadequate wages and/or large families; Fatherless families. What do a, b, c, d and e stand for?

Answers (to be revealed by the tutor)

a = Inadequate wages and/or large families
b = Old age
c = Fatherless families
d = Sickness
e = Unemployment

Source: Haralambos (1980, p.147).

Advantages of this activity

1. It is a type of 'game', and this always creates a refreshing atmosphere.
2. Key issues will have been discussed in the small-group session, and debate will also be provoked by the revelation of the answers (and the comparison of student responses with the real figures).

Potential problem

Statistics are always viewed as complex, and a complex-sounding game can complicate things even further! Thus, the whole exercise has to be explained in simple terms!

Main learning outcome

Students will be engaged by numerical data and in the process of understanding statistics and their meaning.

Variation

The names or criteria on the horizontal axis can be taken out, and the same exercise can be carried out in reverse!

65

Accept and reject

In a nutshell

This technique emphasizes the importance of statistical evidence and asks students to weigh up which pieces of evidence they can use and which they would like to dispose of.

Aims

1. To encourage students to think about the meaning and quality of numerical evidence.
2. To provoke discussion about the significance and implications of certain facts and figures.

What is needed

- Six pieces of pre-prepared statistical evidence (on separate pieces of card).
- An envelope wallet.

Time required

10 minutes (small-group work) plus 15 minutes (whole-group discussion).

How it works

The class is split in two. The tutor gives one group of students six specific statistics on six separate pieces of card – statistics which are highly relevant to a key debate that they are studying. This group has to pick out three statistics to help them argue one 'line' in the debate. They retain their selected three statistics and put the three statistics which they rejected into a 'wallet'. This wallet is handed to the other student subgroup who are asked to develop a line of thought using the three rejected statistics. Whichever statistics are accepted or rejected, each student group should be able to put forward a 'position' and engage in a debate. After the two main arguments have been put forward (both having been founded directly on the 'accepted' and 'rejected' statistics), a short whole-group discussion could round off the exercise.

A good example in action: Politics – what are the social and economic effects of immigration into France?

The six pieces of evidence for the groups to consider are as follows:

1. 81 per cent of French people say that Spanish immigrants in France are well integrated.
2. 62 per cent of Frenchmen say that the level of French immigration is too high.
3. 23 per cent of Algerians would not want their daughter to marry a young Frenchman.
4. 25 per cent of Portuguese immigrants want to stay in France indefinitely.
5. 60 per cent of all immigrants say that they do not desire French nationality.
6. 78 per cent of North African immigrants say that they do not desire French nationality.

Source: A Hargreaves, *Immigration in Post-War France,* 1987.

Advantages of this activity

1. It encourages students to prioritize and consider statistical evidence itself, and how such evidence relates to, and substantiates, academic arguments.
2. The 'wallet' containing rejected evidence adds an element of suspense!

Potential problem

Students may be nonplussed by the pieces of evidence and might wonder how the figures relate at all to the debate under consideration; they must be encouraged to think purposefully about this!

Main learning outcome

Students will have to discuss and formulate a distinct argument on the basis of three significant statistics.

66

Vox pop

In a nutshell

This activity attempts to engage students in the 'process' of vox pops, straw polls and opinion polls. A vox pop is conducted in class, with all students having a set role to play.

Aims

1. To make students more aware of vox pops and opinion polls – how they operate, how people react to them, and the problems associated with them.
2. To create a role-play situation in which students, with set roles to play, have to think about how respondents in certain situations and under certain circumstances would think, and what opinions they would hold.

What is needed

*   An opinion poll about contemporary issues, to be prepared by the students themselves in the first 20 minutes of the session.
*   Sheets of A3 paper.
*   Felt-tip marker pens.
*   Blu-tack.

Time required

20 minutes (to design the opinion poll) plus 15 minutes (for the opinion poll to be answered) plus 15 minutes (general discussion).

How it works

The whole class decides on a set of pertinent and topical questions that respondents, in a specific country, might be asked by pollsters. After deliberation, three key questions are formulated, written up on separate A3 sheets of paper and attached to the wall for all the students to see. The class is then divided into three subgroups, each representing a different 'voter' and each with a different history (all information supplied by the tutor).

Each subgroup then has to discuss how it, as the person it represents, would respond to each of the three questions. It writes down its responses on a Post-it note and, at the end of the small-group session, places its answers on the wall next to the relevant question. A whole-group discussion then follows on why certain people respond in different ways to the same question.

A good example in action: Media Studies – newspaper and TV preferences

Possible 'identities' for subgroups could be as follows:

- **Group A**: John, 65, ex-City company chairman, annual salary: £90,000, MCC member, eight grandchildren, lives in Surrey.
- **Group B**: Steve, 22, welder, soccer fan, union representative, previously unemployed for two years, girlfriend is a model, lives in Oldham.
- **Group C**: Eleanor, 18, student at Bristol University (ranked fourth best university in country), wants to be a lawyer, divorced parents aged 37 and 39, on full grant, comes from Reading.

Possible questionnaire questions could be as follows:

1. Which newspaper do you read? Why?
2. Which TV programmes, and TV stations, do you most regularly watch?
3. Would you pay for cable TV?

How would these three people be likely to respond to the three questions above? What factors would influence their responses? What is the broader significance of their answers? How could this exercise be expanded and how could the resulting data be collated?

Advantages of this activity

1. It brings the mechanics of vox pops and opinion polls alive.
2. The role-play element of the exercise fosters empathy.
3. Good debate is stimulated both in the small-group context and when the different respondents' views are shared.

Potential problem

Students might want to know more about their group 'identity'. It should be explained that the whole idea of the activity is that they have to deduce, and speculate on, attitudes and opinions knowing only minimal details about their own character.

Main learning outcomes

Students will become familiar with the opinion poll industry 'from the inside', and will be able to discuss the many important issues involved.

Variation

Role-play an election, using the same general formula.

67

Dream statistics

In a nutshell

This is an open-ended, but highly stimulating, activity. It encourages students to think about the different types, and various meanings, of statistics.

Aims

1. To present and discuss data in an imaginative way.
2. To provoke students into thinking about the nature of statistics, and how they are determined.

What is needed

● Three pieces of card.
● Felt-tip marker pens.

Time required

15 minutes (small-group discussion) plus 10 minutes (whole-group discussion).

How it works

Three student subgroups are asked to 'create' three statistics to help them reinforce a key argument that is being analysed in the context of an important academic debate. The statistics have to be (a) 'believable', in the sense of being plausible and

(b) 'convincing', in that the figure backs up the argument that is being pursued. Each group writes its 'dream statistics' on to a piece of card, and then passes it on for another group to consider, analyse and, most importantly, judge.

A good example in action: Law – legal aid

The argument that has to be reinforced is: 'Legal aid is a vital feature of democracy and of a decent, civilized society.'

The 'believable' statistics created (in three different categories) are as follows:

1. 36 per cent of all legal cases in 1992 were brought using legal aid.
2. 76 per cent of all cases brought with the help of legal aid were successful to some degree.
3. Eight EU countries have a recognized legal aid system.

The plausibility of these 'dream statistics' – and how the statistics relate to the above argument – can then be discussed.

Advantages of this activity

1. It forces students to hypothesize and think intelligently about statistics.
2. It can provoke excellent discussion on the nature of statistics.

Potential problem

Students may be slightly confused about the words 'plausible' and 'convincing' – these two key words need to be discussed prior to the exercise.

Main learning outcome

Students will be compelled to think about issues and numbers, and the relationship between the two.

68

Blank-out!

In a nutshell

This strategy is designed to test students' knowledge and their general understanding of a numbers-oriented topic. The tutor's task is to 'blank out' some key figures in a table of statistics – or even blank out all the statistics in a table. The students are then asked to make informed predictions about what the figures should really be.

Aims

1. To make the study of statistics more enjoyable and more 'fun'.
2. To increase students' confidence by getting them to predict, in an informed manner, the blanked-out figures.

What is needed

Copies of statistics, with key figures blanked out.

Time required

15 minutes (small-group discussion about the statistics) plus 15 minutes (whole-group discussion).

How it works

The tutor Tippexes out some or all the numbers in a given table of, say, opinion poll, electoral or economic data and inserts letters in their place. The titles of the two axes are kept visible. The students, in pairs or groups of three, are asked to use their knowledge and judgement to replace the 'letters' with their own informed predictions. The tutor then reveals the correct statistics. This leads to a very interesting whole-group discussion about the accuracy of the predictions, and on what basis all the predictions – whether accurate or inaccurate – were made.

A good example in action: Sociology – class in twentieth-century Britain

Class	1913–31	1932–47
Professional, high managerial and large proprietors	a	b
Lower professional and managerial	7	18
White-collar	c	d
Self-employed (including farmers)	e	5
Supervisors of manual work	f	g
Skilled manual workers	1	h
Semi-skilled and unskilled	i	j
Agricultural workers (including smallholders without employees)	1	k

Source: Karabel and Halsey, cited in Haralambos (1980, p.220).

Students have to insert numbers (for the letters a–k) on the basis of discussion and informed prediction.

The answers are as follows: a=15; b=27; c=4; d=6; e=3; f=2; g=4; h=2; i=1; j=2; k=2. (The tutor reveals these after the students have made predictions for each letter.)

Advantages of this activity

1. The suspense and puzzle-type nature of this exercise stimulates the students.
2. Students are encouraged to engage in discussion – in both the small- and whole-group contexts.

Potential problem

This is a complex activity which needs to be explained in simple terms.

Main learning outcome

Students will be encouraged to think for themselves and develop authoritative predictions based on what they already know.

69

Bogus statistics

In a nutshell

Hand out a table of data with one or several 'bogus' statistics included. Ask the students to identify the rogue figures, and use this 'game' as a prelude to discussion about the nature of statistics.

Aims

1. To encourage students to exploit their own innate knowledge and 'predict' data in an informed, authoritative manner.
2. To create stimulating discussion on an important topic by means of a brief 'game'.

What is needed

Copies of the data (in which plausible, but 'bogus', statistics have replaced the real ones.

Time required

15 minutes (small-group discussion) plus 10 minutes (whole-group discussion).

How it works

Before the class session the tutor retypes a table of data, including in it one or two pieces of bogus data (care should be taken, in some instances, to ensure that, where necessary, the retyped lines still add up to 100 per cent or the equivalent). The students are divided into small groups, each of which is given a copy of the retyped statistics. Their task is to deduce which statistic or statistics are 'bogus' and to circle each doctored statistic. The tutor eventually reveals the offending statistics and leads a whole-group discussion on why the subgroups circled certain figures, and for what correct or incorrect reasons.

A good example in action: History – European economic trends

Output of pig-iron, 1820–1910 (selected countries): Annual production in million metric tons						
	Country					
Year	UK	France	Belgium	Germany	Italy	Russia
1820	0.4	0.2	–	0.1	–	0.1
1850	2.3	0.4	0.1	0.2	–	0.2
1880	9.7	3.7	2.6	4.7	–	2.4
1910	10.2	4.0	1.9	14.8	0.3	5.0

Source: Cook and Stevenson (1992, p.249).

Students have to decide which row or column is made up entirely of bogus figures, and the correct answer is row 3 (1880). The figures should read UK 7.7; France 1.7; Belgium 0.6; Germany 2.7; Italy 0; Russia 0.4 (each figure was inflated by 2m metric tons).

Advantages of this activity

1. It takes the form of an enjoyable puzzle, which can reveal important themes.
2. Students have to use their intelligence and insight to deduce the correct answers.

Potential problem

As with all statistics 'games' the intricacies are easily misunderstood!

Main learning outcome

Students will use their knowledge to justify their decisions and account for the difference between real and bogus statistics.

Variation

Just retype one or two statistics – and not a whole row or column.

70

Invent a political party!

In a nutshell

Enter the world of make-believe by asking students to 'invent' their own political party solely on the basis of a series of (unrelated) statistics. The political party should be designed *just* to win elections, and *just* to gain power. How would this 'new' party gain maximum support from all classes? What would be the party's political agenda?

Aims

1. To stretch students' imaginations and knowledge.
2. To stimulate discussion in buzz groups and in the class as a whole.

What is needed

●   A set of 'helpful' statistics, to be given to each student subgroup.
●   Sheets of A3 paper.
●   Felt-tip marker pens.
●   Blu-tack.

Time required

15 minutes (in subgroups) plus 15 minutes (whole-group discussion).

How it works

The students are divided into groups of six. Each has to construct a political party solely to win elections and gain power. Each group has to create a ten-point manifesto for its party, based, crucially, on a range of statistics (perhaps opinion poll and electoral data) which the tutor gives to each group. The students might also be asked to predict how their new party would fare in the early opinion polls, how much support it could ultimately attract, and where its support would come from. Each group writes its manifesto on a sheet of A3 paper, attaches it to the wall and then presents its thoughts and findings to the class as a whole. This process will naturally lead into a fascinating whole-group discussion.

A good example in action: Politics

RANDOM STATISTICS GIVEN TO GROUPS	OUR POLITICAL PARTY
1 14% of all British women have a 'positive' view of politicians.	We believe in::
2 Two out of three voters are unhappy with Britain's first-past-the-post electoral system.	* Proportional representation
3 83% of non-Lib Dem voters admired the party's 1997 election campaign.	* A one-penny increase in income tax to pay for education
4 9% of all British men have a 'positive' view of politicians.	* Referenda
5 87% of all British voters say that politicians in all the main parties are out of touch with ordinary citizens.	* A decrease in MP's basic salary

This is one group's effort at creating a manifesto based on the statistics given to it. What issues does this exercise raise?

Advantages of this activity

1. It draws on students' knowledge and insights in a whole range of spheres.
2. It contains a very refreshing and under-utilized 'what if?' element.

Potential problem

It could be viewed as too open-ended and too vague, and students might not see the point of the exercise.

Main learning outcomes

Students will not only be compelled to think and speculate, they also have to justify their decisions to the whole group.

Summary and evaluation

All tutors are agreed that numbers and tables are difficult to teach. Particularly in the humanities and the social sciences, students are often confronted by a daunting array of electoral data, opinion poll findings and tables of economic statistics. Nevertheless, teaching strategies generally remain fairly predictable: 'Here's a copy of the table. Have a look at it, and tell me what you see or what the figures mean.' Surely we can be a little more imaginative?

As this chapter has hopefully shown, numbers and tables can be made interesting and exciting. Indeed, as soon as you start to inject a 'puzzle' element into almost any task, students do tend to sit up and take notice. So, with numerical data it seems that a key principle is to create games and puzzles, and also to ask students to 'predict' figures. This immediately brings competition and rivalry, between student groups and against the tutor who holds the answer.

Although creating puzzles and games out of data is a time-consuming task, and may still leave students daunted and confused, surely it is worth the effort? When transformed into strategies involving bogus numbers, role-play and recognition tests, data has big potential, and numbers can be made interesting and exciting – for students and tutors alike.

References and Further Reading

A Child's Bible (1973), London: Piccolo.

Abrams, M. (1981), *A Glossary of Literary Terms*, London: CBS Publishing.

Andresen, L.W. (1994), *Lecturing To Large Groups*, SEDA Paper 81, April, Birmingham: SEDA.

Chalmers, D. and Fuller, R. (1996), *Teaching for Learning at University*, London: Kogan Page.

Charter of the United Nations and Statute of the International Court of Justice (1994), New York: United Nations.

Cook, C. and Stevenson, J. (1992), *The Longman Handbook of Modern European History 1763–1991*, London: Longman.

Derbyshire, J.D. and Derbyshire, I. (1988), *Politics In Britain*, Cambridge: Chambers.

Dickens, C., *Great Expectations*, Harmondsworth: Penguin Books.

Eysenck, H. (1953), *The Structure of Human Personality*, London: Methuen.

Gibbs, G. (1992), *Discussion with More Students*, Oxford: Polytechnics and Colleges Funding Council, Oxford Centre for Staff Development.

Gibbs, G. and Habeshaw, T. (1990), *253 Ideas for your Teaching*, Worcester: Technical and Educational Services Ltd.

Good News Bible (1987), Swindon: Collins Fontana.

Griffin, R. (1994), *The Nature of Fascism*, London: Routledge.

Habeshaw, S., Gibbs, G. and Habeshaw, T. (1992), *53 Problems with Large Classes*, Worcester: Technical and Educational Services Ltd.

Habeshaw, S., Habeshaw, T. and Gibbs, G. (1992), *53 Interesting Things to do in Your Seminars and Tutorials*, Exeter: Technical and Educational Services Ltd.

Haralambos, M. (1980), *Sociology: Themes And Perspectives*, Slough: University Tutorial Press.

Hardman, J. (ed.) (1991), *The French Revolution*, London: Edward Arnold.

Hargreaves, A. (1987), *Immigration In Post-War France*, London: Methuen.

Hiden, J. (1987), *The Weimar Republic*, Harlow: Longman.

Hornby, N. (1995), *High Fidelity*, London: Victor Gollancz.

Hounsell, D., McCulloch, M. and Scott, M. (1996), *The ASSHE Inventory*, Edinburgh: ASSHE.

Hubbard, R. (1991), *53 Interesting Ways to Teach Mathematics*, Worcester: Technical and Educational Services Ltd.

Jacques, D. (1990), *Small Group Teaching*, SCED Paper 57, July.

Jones, E. and Eyles, J. (1979), *An Introduction to Social Geography*, Oxford: Oxford University Press.

Keeble, R. (1990), *The Newspapers Handbook*, London: Routledge.

Lane, P. (1985), *Europe Since 1945*, London: Batsford Academic.

Laver, J. (1993), *Joseph Stalin*, London: Hodder & Stoughton.

Le Gall, G., 'Presidentielle 1988: "une opinion cristallisée"?', *Revue Politique et Parlementaire*, (934), pp. 20–27.

MacArthur, M. (ed.) (1993), *The Penguin Book of Twentieth-Century Speeches*, London: Penguin Books.

Maile, R. (1982), *Economics*, London: Letts.

Mazey, S. (1988), 'The 1988 Presidential Election: First Opening to the Centre', *Politics*, **8**(2).

McCauley, M. (1983), *Stalin and Stalinism*, Harlow: Longman.

McCauley, M. (1987), *The Origins of the Cold War*, Harlow: Longman.

McKie, D. (ed.) (1992), *The Election*, London: Fourth Estate.

Partners in Learning (1996), May–September.

Plumb, J. (1966), *England In The Eighteenth Century (1714–1815)*, London: Penguin Books.

Rhodes, A. (1976), *Propaganda: The Art of Persuasion*, London: Angus & Robertson.

Rushdie, S. (1983), *Shame*, London: Picador.

The Salt Programme (1996), July–September, Milton Keynes: Scripture Union.

The Salt Programme: 11–13+ and all Ages (1997), April–June, Milton Keynes: Scripture Union.

Thomson, R. (1968), *The Pelican History of Psychology*, London: Pelican.

University of Huddersfield Seminar Packs: Division of History, Division of Politics, Division of Sociology, Division of Economics.

von Beyne, K. (ed.) (1988), *Right-wing Extremism in Western Europe*, London: Cass.

Watson, J. (1974), *Twentieth-Century World Affairs*, London: Murray.

Weigall, D. and Kirby, A. (1984), *History Document Questions*, London: Letts.

Student Skills SkillPack Masters

Sue Drew and Rosie Bingham

The Masters are available in the original 12 subject areas:

- Identifying Strengths, Improving Skills
- Organising Yourself and Your Time
- Note Taking*
- Gathering and Using Information
- Essay Writing
- Report Writing
- Oral Presentation
- Group Work
- Solving Problems
- Negotiating and Assertiveness
- Coping with Pressure
- Revising and Examination Techniques

plus two new topics currently available exclusively as SkillPack Masters:

- Confidence with Numbers
- Reflecting on Your Experience*

Each pack consists of:

- a licence – valid for a year – to make unlimited copies of each SkillPack
- guidance of how and when to use the SkillPacks to best effect
- details of the learning outcomes for your chosen SkillPack(s)
- a set of A4 photocopiable masters for the Starter Level SkillPack for your chosen skill
- a set of A4 photocopiable masters for the Development Level SkillPack for your chosen skill*

* *Note Taking* and *Reflecting on Your Experience* are only available at Starter Level

The Student Skills Guide

Sue Drew and Rosie Bingham

This paperback workbook for students covers the original 12 key skill areas. The interactive style is designed to help raise self-awareness. Students can either work through each chapter at the Starter and then the Development Level, or choose a chapter relevant to their current activity.

The book is designed as a textbook and is available as an inspection copy for adoption consideration.

Student Skills Tutor's Handbook

Sue Drew and Rosie Bingham

This large format paperback contains the full text of the SkillPacks in the original 12 subject areas (but not the licence to photocopy them), together with guidance on how and when to use the SkillPacks to best effect.

Student IT Skills

Mark Pettigrew and David Elliott

This book presents a completely new approach to learning and developing IT skills. It is based on experience of how people really learn, has been tested with real students and then rewritten to take their observations into account.

Readers are encouraged to learn IT by doing and by guided exploration, and build their confidence to explore and develop further. They are helped to:

- choose relevant and suitable real world tasks
- find out how their software, whatever it is, can perform the tasks
- increase their confidence in the use of IT
- further develop their IT skills by exploration.

As readers explore, they are encouraged to develop a framework of understanding. The practical skills, along with this framework, form a powerful, self-reinforcing way of learning about IT.

The Student Guide to Making an Oral Presentation

Sue Drew and Richard Gibson

All your students need to know about making a successful presentation.

It can come as a shock for students to find out just how difficult it can be to get up and be at their best in front of a group of critical listeners.

Suddenly your mind goes blank, your palms sweat and your knees shake. This kind of nervous fear can only be tackled by being fully prepared and having thought through all the possibilities. This CD-ROM will take students carefully and rigorously through every step necessary for them to deliver a successful presentation.

Many courses require students to make oral presentations. The points that are lost or won during this very personal and stressful ordeal can result in either a fail or pass in the final assessment. It is crucial that your students are able to use their presentation skills to their very best advantage. This CD-ROM will ensure that they do.

The Student Guide to Making an Oral Presentation can help your students in the following ways:

- It is divided into clear, manageable sections. This makes the process of preparation and delivery clear and easy to understand, encouraging confidence.
- The package is very interactive, encouraging students to type in notes and think about what they are doing.
- The assistance provided is entirely practical, helping students make the best preparations for their particular presentation.
- The wide range of video clips and speakers helps attract and hold attention. They clarify how, and how not, to make the best of a presentation.
- The process of preparation is easy to follow, enabling students to go at their own pace and make notes they can save for reference later. It is easy to restart where they left off.
- All angles of making a presentation are covered, ensuring that every student will find something of interest and use.
- All the material can be covered in an hour; or it can be split up into separate sections. Students can use the CD for reference or as a self-contained tutorial.
- Teachers and lecturers might find it a useful basis for class discussions and activities.
- Unrestricted use. There is no licence involved.

Minimum requirements: Windows 95 with speakers or headphones.

Developing Student Support Groups

A Tutor's Guide

Rosie Bingham and Jaquie Daniels

This practical guide offers information and ideas which will help you set up and maintain student support groups. The rapid changes taking place in Further and Higher Education have included the growing demand for students to be offered more flexible learning while tutors are required to cover the same amount of material in less contact time, as well as fostering the personal and professional development of individual students. The emphasis on encouraging independent learning may leave some students feeling isolated and dissatisfied with their learning experience. Student support groups are increasingly being used to address some of these challenges. Such groups facilitate team working and also offer personal and social support, and development for the individuals involved.

This guide has been written in an interactive format which will help the reader work through the issues involved in establishing student support groups. These include:

- What is the purpose of a student support group?
- How will it be structured?
- How will you monitor and support the group?
- What are the potential difficulties?
- Will you use assessment with the group and if so, how?

Developing Student Support Groups is based upon Sheffield Hallam University tutors' experience of working with support groups and is a tried and tested method of working.

Gower

The Management of a Student Research Project

Second Edition

John A Sharp and Keith Howard

Endorsed by The Open University

This book is a practical guide for all those students intending to write up and present for examination the results of research projects. It assumes that most students in this situation will be depending largely on their own resources. It shows them how to manage the project within a set period of time and with limited facilities. In particular, it considers how the project can best be managed to maximise the chances of success; provides a step-by-step guide from initial selection and justification of the topic through to final presentation of the research findings; and discusses research methods and tools.

Your Student Research Project

Martin Luck

Now that you are approaching the final stages of your degree, have you ever wondered how you're going to cope with writing your dissertation? Apart from the practicalities of suddenly having to think and work in a completely different, and more in-depth, way than ever before, how are you going to fit it in with the rest of your work and also have a social life? *Your Student Research Project* will show you how.

This book gives you practical advice on how to cope with your project and make a success of your studies. It is written in clear, accessible language; provides a clear outline of practical guidance on how to run your project, from thinking about what topic to cover to the most effective way of presenting it; explains how to work with your supervisor and the other important people around you; shows you how to squeeze the maximum value from the effort you put in; enables you to recognize how you have changed in the process; and encourages you to exploit the skills and experiences you have gained in the world beyond your degree.

It takes a different approach to other books on research methods because it considers the project as only one part of your existence. It concentrates on advice, ideas and examples while still giving thought to how you will manage your work within a crowded and exciting life. Above all, *Your Student Research Project* helps you to keep track of where you are heading and to make the right preparations for the future.

Gower